Decorative Brai

Milanese Lace

MW00825065

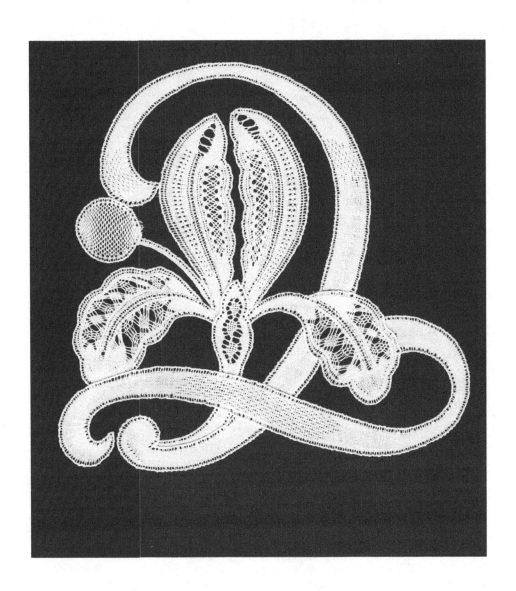

Patricia Read, Lucy Kincaid & Jane Read

Decorative Braids for Milanese Lace

Copyright © 2021 Patricia Read, Lucy Kincaid & Jane Read

All rights reserved. This book or any portion thereof may not be reproduced or used in any manner whatsoever without the express written permission of the publisher except for the use of brief quotations in a book review.

ISBN:
978-1-80227-147-8 (Paperback)
978-1-80227-148-5 (eBook)

Contents

CONTENTS

Introduction

The decorative braids of Milanese lace have proved ideal for incorporation into modern and contemporary as well as traditional lace. For the authors, it has been exciting to see the new directions in which modern lace has moved.

The original books, 'Milanese Lace: An Introduction' and 'New Braids and Designs in Milanese Lace', both by Read and Kincaid (1988; 1994), have been out of print for many years. In this volume, we have gathered together the thirty braids from the first book and the forty-one braids from the second book, and added nearly fifty braids to them, not previously published.

This is intended to be a reference book, and it is hoped that it will bring Milanese decorative braids to a new audience and further stimulate creativity, encouraging lacemakers to develop new designs for the modern world.

Happy lacemaking.

References

Read, Patricia, and Kincaid, Lucy, 1988. *Milanese Lace: An Introduction*. Batsford, ISBN 0 7134 5707 4

Read, Patricia, and Kincaid, Lucy, 1994. *New Braids and Designs in Milanese Lace*. Batsford, ISBN 0 7134 7192 1

Read, Pat. 2008. *An introduction to Milanese Lace*. The Lace Guild, ISBN 1-901372-24-3

Abbreviations

cls, ws	cloth stitch or whole stitch
edge st	cloth stitch worker with edge pair, twist both pairs twice, pin inside both pairs
hs	half stitch
lt	left
pr, prs	pair, pairs
rep, rept	repeat
rt	right
st	stitch
thro	through
ts	turning stitch (indicated on the diagrams with an o)
tw	twist
W, Ws	weavers, workers or leaders
x t	cross turn (half stitch)
x t x	cross turn cross (cloth or whole stitch)
x t t	cross turn turn

Some Notes

Some braids lend themselves to turning curves graciously, in particular all the meandering braids and the figure of eights. Within each repeat (as necessary), work an extra turn on the outside of the curve to help ease the braid round.

Many braids, such as bubbles, ovals, pearl and others, can be used in very narrow trails by omitting some of the outer, straight passives.

A few braids, such as grenades, can be narrowed by reducing the number of grenades across the work.

Note that the arosa pattern only shows up when the fabric is dense. Use more bobbins than you think you need.

Colour

More and more people are incorporating colour into their lace. Here, the world is your oyster! Colour can be used to follow the braid, in which case the effect is often random as the workers and passives exchange places. This can be controlled by using an extra twist within a cloth stitch to send the colour in the direction of your choice. Colour can be used to highlight certain aspects of the braid, or the braid can be worked as a single block of colour. The choices are endless and only limited by the worker's creativity.

Braids

AMMONITE
15 prs

The decoration in this braid will show best when the pattern is tightly curved, as here. Blind pins should be used as necessary when working the inside of the curve. These have been indicated on the sample pattern.

*Work 2 rows cls. Leave W on inside of curve.

Tw twice 5 passive pairs on outside of curve, tw once next 5 passive pairs, leave untwisted the last 2 passive prs (on inside of curve).*

Rep from * to * for desired length.

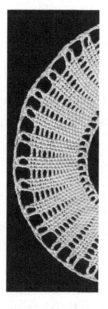
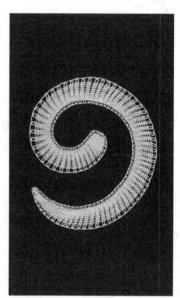

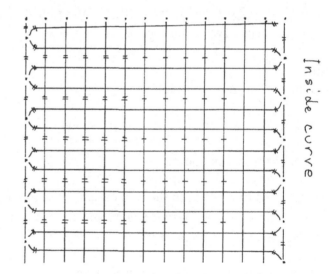

Inside curve

1

ANGELS

14 prs

Ts with W and centre pr.

Lt W cls to lt thro 5 prs, tw W twice, edge st and pin. Leave. Work rt W to rt in similar manner.

Centre 6 prs:
Tw each pr once.

* Centre 4 prs:
Cross 2 lt prs thro 2 rt prs in cls. Lt 2 prs work 1 cls and rt 2 prs also work 1 cls.

Left side:
W thro 2 prs, tw W once, cls and tw thro next pr, cls thro next pr, ts with next pr, return thro 1 pr, tw W once, cls and tw thro next pr, cls thro 2 prs, tw W twice, edge st and pin. W thro 1 pr in cls. Leave. Tw the next pr once.

Right side:
Work in similar manner to lt side.

Cross 2 centre lt prs thro 2 centre rt prs in cls.

Tw each of these 4 prs once.

Work the lt of these 4 prs to the lt in cls and tw thro 2 prs, cls thro 2 more prs, tw W twice, edge and pin. W thro 1 pr in cls. Leave. Tw next pr once.

Work the centre lt pr to the lt in cls and tw thro 3 prs, cls thro 2 prs, tw W twice, edge st and pin.

Work the rt side in a similar manner.*

Rep from * to * for desired length.

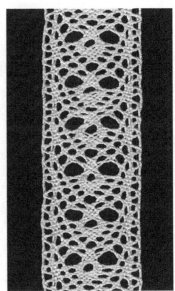

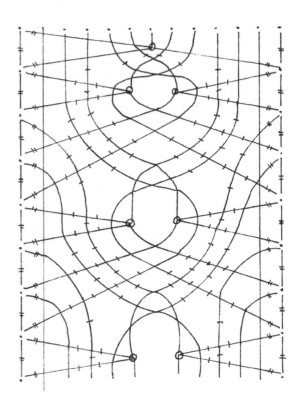

ARCHWAY
14 prs

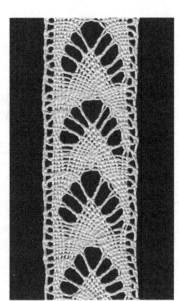

* Ts with W and centre pr. Cls is used throughout.

Left side:
Work lt pr of the centre 2 prs thro 5 prs to lt, tw W twice, edge st and pin.

Work W thro 5 prs, leave W and take last pr passed thro as new W and return thro 4 prs, tw W twice, edge st and pin.

Work W thro 4 prs, leave W and take last pr passed thro as new W and return thro 3 prs, tw W twice, edge st and pin.

Work W thro 3 prs, leave W and take last pr passed thro as new W and return thro 2 prs, tw W twice, edge st and pin. Work W thro 2 prs. Leave.

Right side:
Work in similar manner to lt side.

Centre 8 prs:
Tw each pr 3 times.

Cross lt 4 prs thro rt 4 prs in ws.

New W will be the 2nd passive pr on the side of braid with next pinhole to be worked.

The pattern may be repeated from *, but one or more rows of cls may be worked before the archway is repeated. In the sample shown, 1 row of cls was worked.

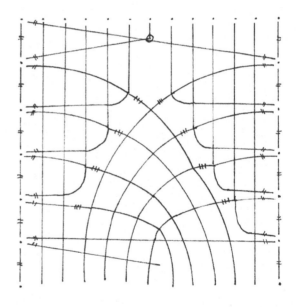

AROSA

15 prs

Work in cls throughout.

W thro 1 pr, tw W once, (thro 2 prs, tw W once). Rep 4 more times, W thro 1 pr, tw W twice, edge st and pin.

Rep this row once in the opposite direction.

W thro 1 pr, tw W once, thro 1 pr, tw W once, *thro 2 prs, tw W once*. Rep from * to * twice more. W thro 1 pr, tw W once, thro 1 pr, tw W twice, edge st and pin.

Rep this row once in the opposite direction. #

Rep from # to #.

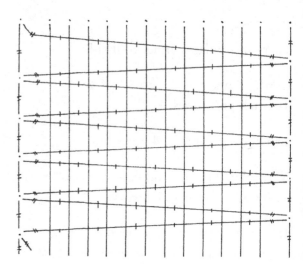

ASTER
14 prs

Work in cls throughout.

Work ts with W and centre pr. These 2 prs are now Ws. Work lt W to lt thro 3 prs, tw W once, thro 2 prs, tw W twice, edge st and pin. Work rt W to rt in similar manner.

*Centre 2 prs:
Work together in cls (no twist).

Left side:
W thro 2 prs, tw W once, thro 2 prs, ts with next pr, return to lt edge with lt pr thro 2 prs, tw W once, thro 2 prs, tw W twice, edge st and pin.

Right side:
Work in similar manner to lt side.

Centre 2 prs:
Work together in cls.

Left side:
W thro 2 prs, tw W once, thro 3 prs. Leave.

Right side:
Work in similar manner to lt side.

Centre 2 prs:
Work together in cls. (Ws have changed sides)

Left side:
Work lt W to lt thro 3 prs, tw W once, thro 2 prs, tw W twice, edge st and pin.

Right side:
Work in similar manner to lt side.*

Rep from * to *.

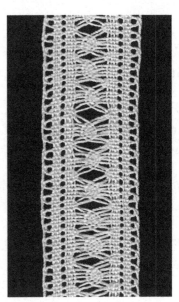

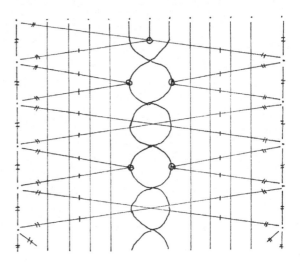

BASKETWEAVE

14 prs

Work 1 row of cls thro 11 prs, tw W twice, edge st and pin with last pr. Leave.

* Take next 2 passive prs, cls. Leave. Continue in this manner thro 8 more prs of passives, leaving 1 passive pr and edge pr unworked.

Work W thro in cls. Tw W twice, edge st and pin with last pr. Leave.*

Rep from * to * for desired length.

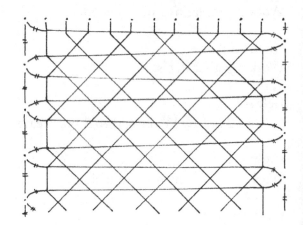

BEADS
14 prs

Work ts with W and centre pr. Both these pairs are Ws and they work in cls throughout.

Work lt W to lt thro 5 prs, tw W twice, edge st and pin. Leave.

Work rt W to rt in similar manner.

*Centre 4 prs:
Work 1 cls with 2 lt prs and 1 cls with 2 rt prs.

Cross the 2 lt prs thro the 2 rt prs in cls.

Work 1 cls with the 2 lt prs and 1 cls with the 2 rt prs.

Left side:
W thro 3 prs, tw W once, thro 1 more pr, ts with next pr. Return thro 1 pr, tw W once, thro 3 prs, tw W twice, edge st and pin. Leave.

Right side:
Work in similar manner to lt side.*

Rep from * to * for desired length, finishing with the crossing of the 4 centre prs.

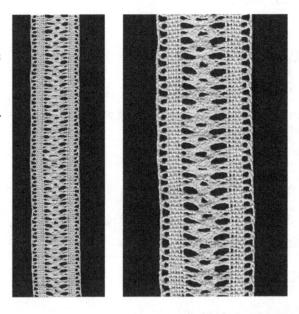

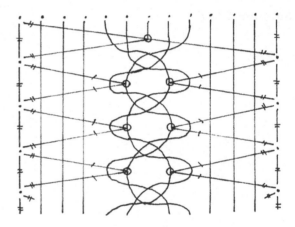

BRICK - 1
14 prs

Work in cls throughout.

* Work W thro 4 prs, tw W twice, thro 3 prs, tw W twice, thro 4 prs, tw W twice, edge st and pin.*

Rep from * to * twice more.

Tw every passive pr once.

** Work W thro 3 prs, tw W twice, thro 5 prs, tw W twice, thro 3 prs, tw W twice, edge st and pin.**

Rep from ** to ** twice more.

Tw every passive pr once. #

Rep from # to #.

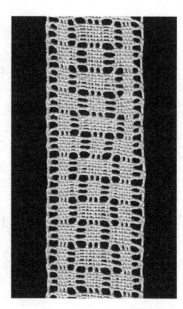

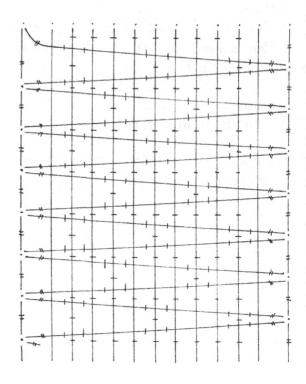

BRICK - 2
15 prs

Work in cls throughout.

* Work W thro 4 prs, tw W twice, thro 4 prs, tw W twice, thro 4 prs, tw W twice. Edge st and pin.*

Rep from * to * once more.

Tw all 12 passive prs once.

** W thro 3 prs, tw W twice, thro 6 prs, tw W twice, thro 3 prs, edge st and pin.**

Rep from ** to ** once more.

To make the hole:

W thro 3 prs, tw W twice, thro 2 prs, tw the next 2 prs once, work one ts with the Ws and next pr, W thro 3 prs, tw W twice, thro 3 prs, edge st and pin.

Rep from ** to ** once. #

Repeat from # to #.

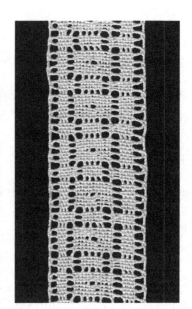

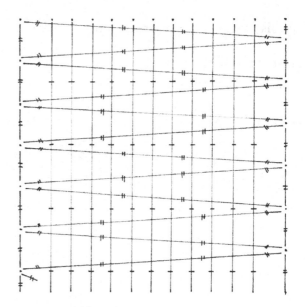

BRICK - 3

14 prs

Tw the centre 9 passive prs once.

* W thro 1 pr in cls, tw W once, cls and tw thro 1 pr, cls thro 3 prs, tw W once, thro 1 pr in cls and tw, thro 3 prs in cls, tw W once, thro 1pr in cls and tw, thro 1 pr in cls, tw W twice, edge st and pin.

Rep this row in the opposite direction.

Centre 9 passive prs:
Tw all untwisted prs once.

W thro 1 pr in cls, tw W once, thro 1 pr in cls and tw, thro 3 prs in cls, tw W once, thro 1 pr in cls and tw, thro 2 prs in cls, tw W once, thro 1 pr in cls, tw W twice, edge st and pin.

Rep this row in the opposite direction.

Centre 9 passive prs:
Tw all untwisted prs once.*

Rep from * to *.

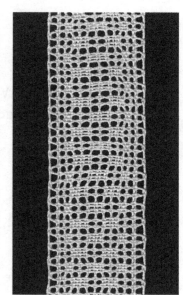

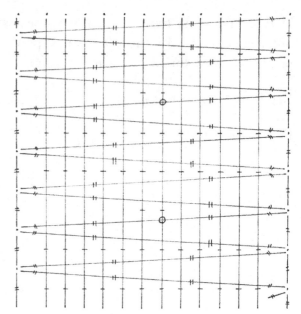

BUBBLES
14 prs

Work in cls throughout

Work ts with W and centre pr. Both these prs are now Ws. Work lt W to lt thro 2 prs, tw W twice, thro 1 pr, tw W once, thro 2 prs, tw W twice, edge st and pin. Leave. Work rt W to the rt in similar manner. Leave.

* Centre 4 prs:
Ts with 2 lt prs.
Ts with 2 rt prs.
Using each pr as 1 thread, work 1 cls.
Using thread singly: ts with 2 lt prs and ts with 2 rt prs.
These are called the PLAIT PAIRS.

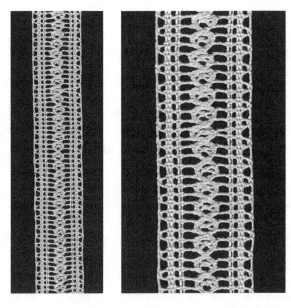

Lt W thro 2 prs, tw W once, thro next pr, tw W twice, then 1 cls thro the 2 plait prs using each of these 2 prs as 1 thread, tw W 3 times.

Rt W thro to lt in a similar manner.

Work cls with the 2 Ws, tw both these prs 3 times. The Ws have now changed sides.

Work ts with each set of plait prs.

Work lt W thro the 2 plait prs using each of these 2 prs as 1 thread, tw W twice, thro next pr, tw W once, thro 2 prs, tw W twice, edge st and pin. Leave.

Work rt W to rt in similar manner.*

Rep from * to * for desired length.

To finish: Work ts with Ws in the centre.

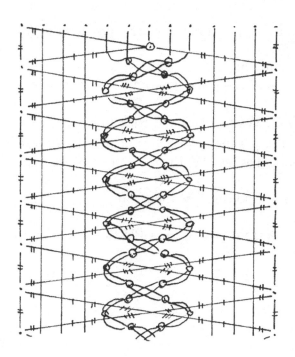

BUDS, 4-Pin and 6-Pin
14 prs

4-Pin Bud (made without pins)

In cls braid:
* W thro 7 prs, work last but one pr passed thro back thro 1 pr.

2 outside prs of these centre 4 prs are Ws.

2 centre prs:
Tw 3 times each, cls and tw 3 times. Leave.

** Work Ws to edges and back (but not thro the centre twisted prs).

Tw Ws 3 times and work them to centre. Tw all 4 prs 3 times each.

2 outside prs of these centre 4 prs are now Ws.

2 centre prs:
Cls and tw 3 times. Leave.*

Work Ws to edges and back to centre, work cls with 2 centre prs (both Ws). Use pr nearest to next hole to be worked as new W. The other pr becomes a passive.**

6-Pin Bud (made without pins)

Work from * to * as for 4-Pin Bud, and then from ** to **.

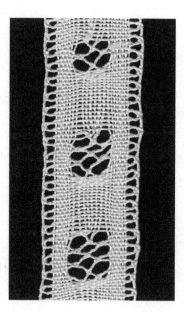

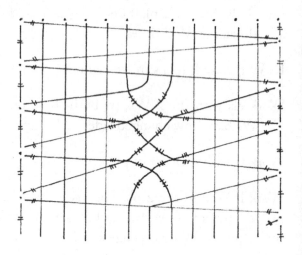

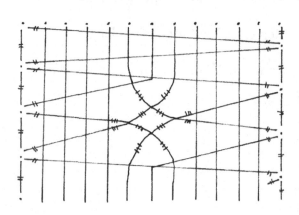

CHEVRON
16 prs

The decoration in this braid will show best when the pattern is tightly curved, as here. If possible, make twice as many pinholes on the outside of the curve (see the sample pattern).

Work a few rows of cls braid. Leave W as a passive pr in the centre. Tw the 5 passive prs on lt twice and the 5 passive prs on rt twice.

* Work the 2 centre lt prs thro the 2 centre rt prs in cls. Work the lt of the 4 centre prs in cls thro 5 prs to lt, tw W twice, edge st and pin. Leave.

Work the lt of the remaining 3 centre prs in cls thro 6 prs to lt, tw W twice, edge st and pin. Leave.

Work the rt of the 2 remaining centre prs thro 5 prs to rt, tw W twice. Leave.

Work the remaining centre pr thro 6 prs to rt, tw W twice, edge st and pin. Leave.

Tw all the passive prs twice.*

Rep from * to * for desired length.

Reverse these instructions if the inside of the curve is on the left.

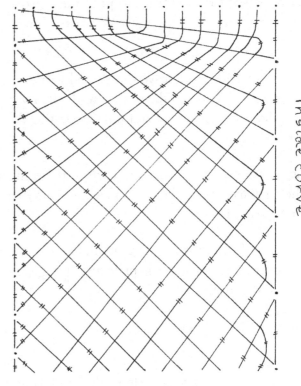

Inside curve

CHICANE

16 prs

Work in cls throughout.

Work tw with W and centre pr. Both these prs are now Ws. Work lt W to the lt thro 6 prs, tw twice, edge st and pin. Work rt W to the rt in similar manner.

Work rt W thro 5 prs to lt, ts with next pr, return with the rt pr thro 5 prs to the rt, tw W twice, edge st and pin. Leave.

Left side:
Work W thro 6 prs to rt, leave the W and work ts with the last pr passed thro and the next pr to the lt, work the lt of these 2 prs thro 4 prs to lt, tw W twice, edge st and pin.

Work W thro 4 prs to rt, leave the W and work ts with the last pr passed thro and the next pr to the lt, work the lt of these 2 prs thro 2 prs to lt, tw W twice, edge st and pin.

Work W thro 2 prs to rt, leave the W and work ts with the last pr passed thro and the next pr to the lt. Tw twice the lt of these 2 prs, edge st and pin. Leave the W and edge pr.

Tw the next 6 prs twice and work each of them in turn thro the 6 passive prs on the rt side. Tw the 6 prs that are now on the rt twice.

* Work the lt W thro the 5 passive prs and make a ts with the 6th pr. Return with the lt pr to the lt edge, tw W twice, edge st and pin.*

Rep from * to * once more.

Right side:
Work ts with W and next pr to lt, work thro 1 more pr. Return with last pr passed thro to rt edge, tw twice, edge st and pin.
Work W thro 2 prs, ts with next pr, thro 1 more pr.
Return with last pr passed thro to rt edge, tw twice, edge st and pin.

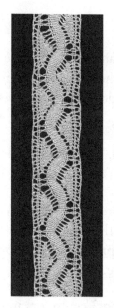
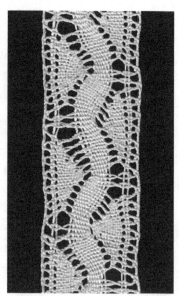

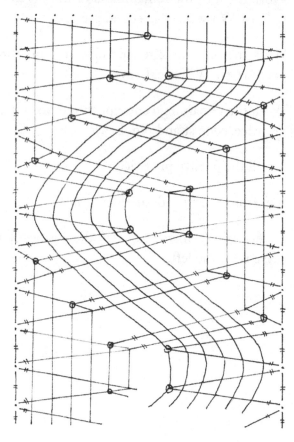

Work thro 4 prs, ts with next pr, thro 1 more pr.

Return with last pr passed thro to rt edge, tw twice, edge st and pin.

Work thro 6 prs, leave W and work ts with the last pr passed thro and the next pr to the rt.

Work the rt of these 2 prs thro 4 prs to rt, tw W twice, edge st and pin.

Work W thro 4 prs, leave W and work ts with the last pr passed thro and the next pr to the rt.

Work the rt of these 2 prs thro 2 prs to the rt, tw W twice, edge st and pin.

Work W thro 2 prs, leave W and work ts with the last pr passed thro and the next pr to the rt, tw twice, edge st and pin. Leave W and edge pr.

Tw the next 6 prs twice and work each of them in turn thro the 6 passive prs on the lt side. Tw the 6 prs that are now on the lt twice.

**Work the rt W thro the 5 passive prs and make a ts with the 6th pr. Return with the rt pr to the rt edge, tw twice, edge st and pin.

Rep from** to ** once more.

Left side:
Work in similar manner to right side.#

Rep from # to # for desired length.

CLOTH DIVISIONS - 1 AND 2

CLOTH DIVISIONS – 1

Any no prs

In cls braid:

Tw the passive prs 3 times.

All the passive prs may be twisted, but if the braid is curved, only some of the passive prs on the outside of the curve need to be twisted.

CLOTH DIVISIONS – 2

14 prs

Leave W at the edge.

* Take next 2 passive prs and work cls and tw (called a "double").

Rep from * twice more.

Three "doubles" have now been worked.

Tw twice next passive pr and work cls with this pr and first pr from the last "double". Leave.

** Work cls with the second pr from this "double" and the first pr from the next "double". Leave.

Rep from ** once more. Tw the remaining pr twice.

Continue working with W.

If the braid is fairly wide, more "doubles" can be made.

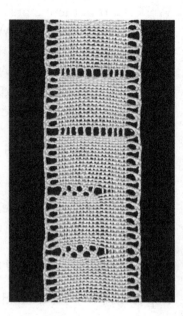

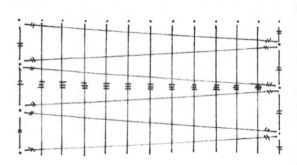

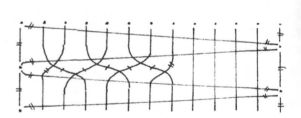

CLOTH DIVISIONS - 3
14 prs

W works in cls throughout.

Work 2 rows.

Next row: work W thro 4 prs. Leave.

Tw remaining 7 passive prs once each. Work W thro these 7 prs, twisting the W once between each pr, but do not tw the passive prs. Tw W twice, edge st and pin. Leave.

* Work next 2 prs in cls. Leave.

Rep from * twice more. Tw next pr once.

Work W thro 6 prs cls and tw. W thro next pr and tw passive pr once. W thro 4 prs, tw W twice, edge st and pin.

Continue working cls braid for desired length. In the sample shown, there are eight rows of cls between the divisions.

The number of crossed prs may be more or less according to the width and curve of the braid and the number of pairs used.

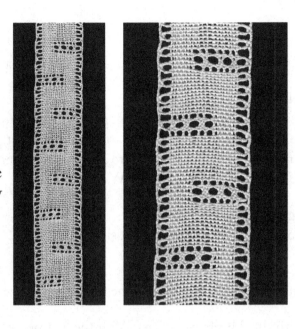

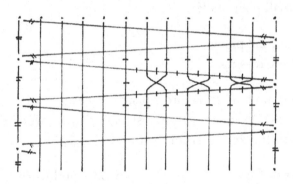

COLLET
14 prs

Work a ts with W and centre pr. Both these prs are now Ws.

Left side:
Work the lt W to lt thro 5 prs, edge st and pin. Work the W to the rt thro 3 prs, tw W once. Leave. Take the last pr past thro as new W and work it to lt thro 2 prs, edge st and pin. Work the W to the rt thro 2 prs, tw W once. Leave.

Right side:
Work in similar manner to left side.

* Centre 4 prs:
Using 2 bobbins together as one thread, work one cls.

With the 2 lt prs work 2 hs. With the 2 rt prs work 2 hs (small plait made).

Centre 8 prs:
The Crossing

2nd pr from lt: cls thro 2 prs, tw once and work small plait (2 hs). With the 2 prs just passed thro, work the same with the 2nd pr from the rt.

1st pr from lt: cls thro 2 prs, tw once and work small plait with the 2 prs passed thro. Work the same with the 1st pr from the rt.

Centre 4 prs:
Work the 2 lt prs thro the 2 rt prs in cls and tw.

Centre 8 prs:

Left side:
Work the 3rd pr from lt thro 2 lt prs in cls, tw once, and work small plait with the 2 prs passed thro.
Work the 4th pr from lt thro 2 lt prs in cl.st, tw once, and work small plait with the 2 prs passed thro.

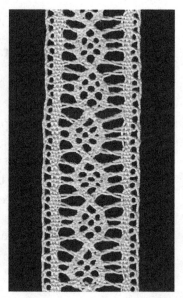

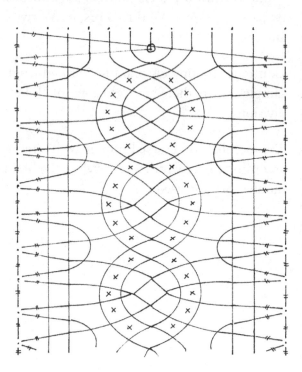

Right side:
Work in similar manner to left side.

Left side:
Work 4th pr from lt to the lt in cls thro 2 prs, edge st and pin. Return thro 2 prs. Leave.
Work 5th pr from lt to the lt in cls thro 3 prs, edge st and pin. Return thro 3 prs, tw it once. Leave.

Right side:
Work in similar manner to left side.*

Work from * to * for desired length.

CRESCENT
14 prs

Work ts with W and centre pr. Both these prs are now Ws and they work in cls throughout.

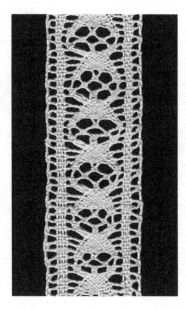

* Left side:
Work lt W to lt thro 3 prs, tw W twice, thro 2 more prs, tw W twice, edge st and pin.

Work W thro 2 prs, tw W twice, thro 1 more pr and ts with next pr. Return with W thro 1 pr, tw W twice, thro 2 more prs, tw W twice, edge st and pin. Leave.

Right side:
Work in similar manner to lt side.

Tw 6 centre prs twice.

Centre 4 prs:
Cross 2 lt prs thro 2 rt prs in cls and tw twice. Leave.

Left side:
Work W thro 2 prs, tw W twice, thro 1 more pr and ts with next pr. Return with W thro 1 pr, tw W twice, thro 2 prs, tw W twice, edge st and pin. Leave.

Right side:
Work in similar manner to lt side.

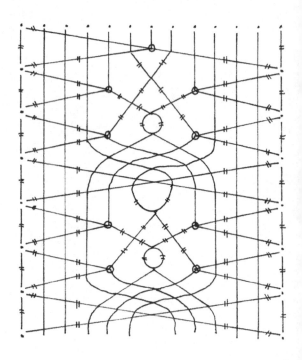

Centre 6 prs (only the centre 2 prs have 2 tw):

Cross lt 3 prs thro rt 3 prs in cls. No tw after the completion of this crossover.

Left side:
W thro 2 prs, tw W twice, thro 3 prs. Leave.

Right side:
W thro 2 prs, tw W twice, thro 4 prs.

The Ws have now changed sides.*

Rep from * to * for desired length.

CROSS-BUD
16 prs

Work in cls braid.

The divisions (which are optional) are made by twisting each passive pr 3 times.

In the next row, work ts with W and centre pr. Both these prs are now Ws.

Left side:
Lt W thro 6 prs to lt, tw W twice, edge st and pin. W thro 6 prs to centre, leave the W. Make a ts with the last pr passed thro and next pr to lt.
Lt of these 2 prs is new W, work it thro 4 prs to lt, tw W twice, edge st and pin.
W thro 3 prs to rt, ts with next pr. Lt of these 2 prs is new W, work it thro 3 prs to lt, tw W twice, edge st and pin. Leave.

Right side:
Work in similar manner to lt side.

Centre 4 prs:
Tw each pr twice.
Work 2 lt prs thro 2 rt prs in cls.
Tw each pr twice.

Left side:
W thro 4 prs, ts with next pr and cls thro next pr. Last pr passed thro is new W, return thro 5 prs, tw W twice, edge st and pin. Leave.

Right side:
Work in same way as lt side.
Work both Ws to centre and make a ts. One pr remains as a passive, and the other is the W.

Continue in cls braid, working at least 5 rows before making divisions or another cross-bud.

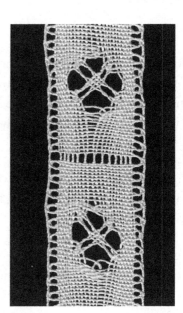

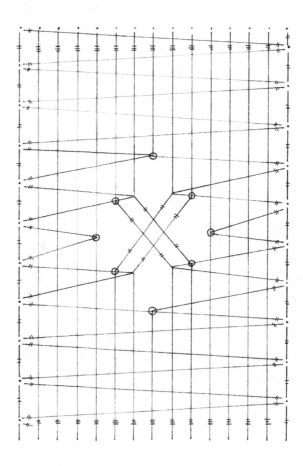

CROSS-NET

14 prs

Work ts with W and centre pr. Both these prs are now Ws. Work the lt W to the lt in cls thro 5 prs, tw twice, edge st and pin, and work the rt W to the rt in a similar manner. Leave. With the 2 centre passive prs work 2 hs (small plait made).

* Left side:
Work W thro 3 prs in cls, ts with next pr, tw rt pr once, and return with lt pr thro 3 prs, tw twice, edge st and pin. W thro 3 prs in cls, tw W once.

Right side:
Work in similar manner to lt side.

Cross-net:
This is made with the centre 6 prs, each twisted once.
Work cls and tw once throughout:
Lt centre pr thro 2 prs to lt.
Rt centre pr thro 2 prs to rt.
Lt centre pr thro 2 prs to rt.
Lt centre pr thro 1 pr to lt.

Centre 2 prs:
Outside lt pr thro 2 prs to rt.
Outside rt pr thro 2 prs to lt.
Two centre prs (cls and tw) twice.
Lt pr thro 3 prs to lt tw W twice, edge st and pin.
Rt pr thro 3 prs to rt tw W twice, edge st and pin.*

Rep from * to * for desired length, finishing with a cross-net.

Note: Pull up the cross-net carefully. If it bunches too tightly, ease it out with a needle pin. Try to keep the cross-nets in line down the centre of the braid.

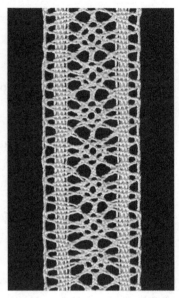

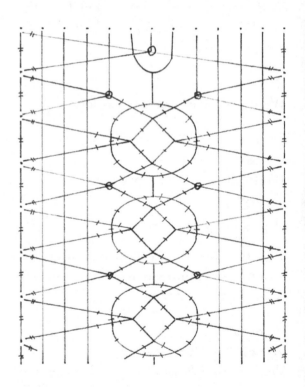

CROSS-OVER - 1
14 prs

Work ts with W and centre pr. Both these prs are now Ws and they work in cls throughout.

Lt W thro 5 prs to lt, tw W twice, edge st and pin. Leave.

Work rt W to rt in similar manner. Leave.

** Left side:
W thro 2 prs, tw W once, cls and tw thro 1 pr, cls thro one more pr, ts with next pr, return thro 1 pr, tw W once, cls and tw thro 1 pr, cls thro 2 prs, tw W twice, edge st and pin. Leave.

Right side:
Work in similar manner to lt side.

Cross the 2 centre lt prs thro the 2 centre rt prs in cls.

Centre 6 prs:
Tw once each pr.
Lt pr cls and tw thro 2 prs to rt.
Rt pr cls and tw thro 3 prs to lt.

Left side:
* W thro 3 prs, ts with next pr, return to lt thro 3 prs, tw W twice, edge st and pin.

Rep from * once more.

Right side:
Work in similar manner to lt side.

Centre 6 prs:
Each pr twisted once.
Work centre lt pr cls and tw thro 2 prs to lt.
Work centre rt pr cls and tw thro 2 prs to rt.

Centre 4 prs:
Cross the 2 lt prs thro the 2 rt prs in cls.**

Rep from ** to ** for desired length, finishing with the crossover of the centre 4 prs.

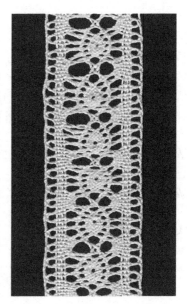

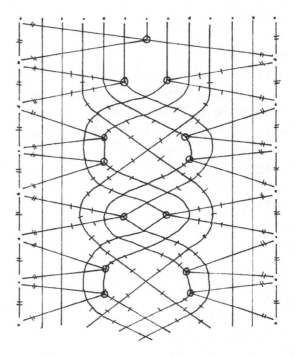

CROSS-OVER - 2
14 prs

Work 1 row of cls, edge st and pin. Leave.
Work one hs with 6th and 7th passive prs.
Work W in cls thro 5 prs, ts with next pr.
These two prs are now Ws and they work in cls throughout.

Work the lt W to the lt thro 5 prs, tw W twice, edge st and pin. Leave.
Work the rt W to the rt in a similar manner. Leave.

Centre 6 prs:
Tw each pr once.
Lt centre pr cls and tw thro lt 2 prs.
Rt centre pr cls and tw thro rt 2 prs.

Centre 4 prs:
Pass lt 2 prs thro rt 2 prs in cls.

Left side:
* Work W thro 2 prs, tw W once, cls and tw thro next pr, cls thro next pr, ts with next pr (put aside the remaining 7 prs). Return with W thro next pr, tw W once, cls and tw thro next pr, thro next 2 prs, tw W twice, edge st and pin.

Rep from * once more. Leave.

Right side:
Work in similar manner to left side.

Centre 4 prs:
Cross 2 lt prs thro 2 rt prs.
Tw these 4 prs once.

Centre 6 prs:
The lt pr and the rt pr each work to centre in cls and tw thro 2 prs and thro each other and remain as the 2 centre prs (no twists on the other 4 prs).

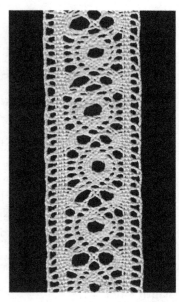

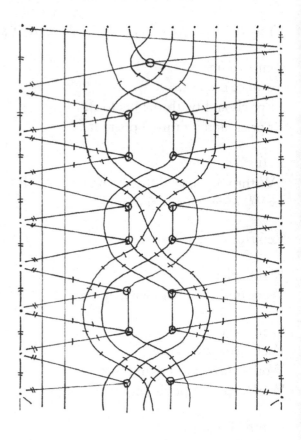

Left side:
** Work W thro 3 prs, ts with next pr (put aside the remaining 8 prs). Return with W thro 3 prs, tw W twice, edge st and pin.

Rep from ** once more. Leave.

Right side:
Work in similar manner to lt side. #

To repeat the whole pattern, work from # to #.

DADO

14 prs

Work in cls throughout.

Work ts with W and centre pr. Both these prs are now Ws.
Work lt W to lt thro 4 prs, tw W once, thro 1 pr, tw W twice,
edge st and pin.
Work rt W to rt in similar manner.

* Centre 4 prs:
Work 2 lt prs thro 2 rt prs in cls.

Centre 8 prs:
2 lt prs cls and tw.
2 rt prs cls and tw.
Work 2 lt prs thro 2 centre lt prs in cls.
Work 2 rt prs thro 2 centre rt prs in cls.

Centre 4 prs:
Tw each pr once.
Work 2 lt prs thro 2 rt prs in cls and tw.

Left side:
W thro 1 pr in cls, tw W once, thro 1 pr, ts with next pr.
Return with lt pr, thro 1 pr, tw W once, thro 1 pr, tw W
twice, edge st and pin.

Right side:
Work in similar manner to lt side.

Centre 8 prs:
Work 2 centre lt prs thro 2 prs to lt and tw the 2 lt prs
once.
Work 2 centre rt prs thro 2 prs to rt and tw the 2 rt prs
once.*

Rep from * to *.

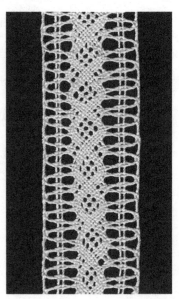

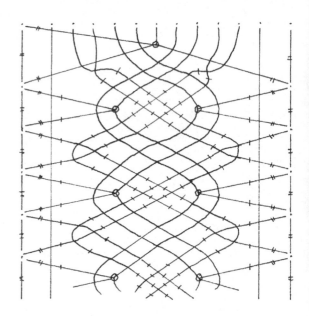

DAISY - 1

16 prs

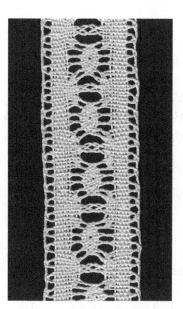

Work in cls throughout.

Work ts with W and centre pr. Both these prs are now Ws. Work lt W to lt thro 6 prs, tw W twice, edge st and pin. Leave. Work rt W to rt in similar manner. Leave.

* Centre 4 prs:
Work 2 lt prs thro 2 rt prs, then tw all 4 prs twice.

Left side:
W thro 4 prs, ts with next pr, cls thro next pr, return with lt pr thro 5 prs, tw W twice, edge st and pin. W thro 6 prs. Leave.

Right side:
Work in similar manner to lt side.

The 2 Ws are now in the centre. Tw each pr once, work cls and tw. Ws have now changed sides.

Left side:
Work lt W thro 6 prs to lt, tw twice, edge st and pin. W thro 6 prs, return with lt pr and make a ts with next pr, lt pr thro 4 prs, tw twice, edge st and pin. W thro 4 prs, tw twice. Leave.

Right side:
Work in similar manner to lt side.

Centre 4 prs:
Tw each pr twice. Work lt 2 prs thro rt 2 prs.
Lt W thro 2 prs to rt.
Rt W thro 2 prs to lt.
Cls with 2 Ws. Ws have changed sides.
Lt W thro 2 prs to lt, tw W twice, thro 4 prs, tw W twice, edge st and pin.
Work rt W to rt in similar manner.*

Rep from * to * for desired length. Finish with the centre crossing of 4 prs.

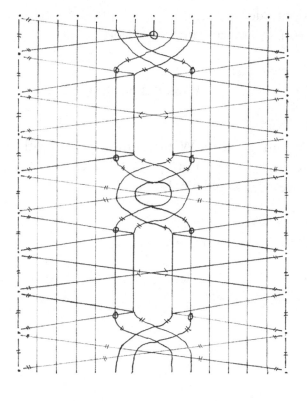

DAISY - 2
16 prs

Work in cls throughout.

Work ts with W and centre pr. Both these prs are now Ws.
Work lt W to lt thro 6 prs, tw W twice, edge st and pin. Leave.
Work rt W to rt in similar manner. Leave.

* Centre 4 prs:
Work lt 2prs thro rt 2 prs, then tw all 4 prs twice.

Left side:
W thro 4 prs, ts with next pr, cls thro next pr, return with lt pr
thro 5 prs, tw W twice, edge st and pin.
W thro 6 prs, return with lt pr, ts with next pr, lt of these 2 prs
thro 4 prs, tw W twice, edge st and pin. Leave.

Right side:
Work in similar manner to lt side.

Centre 4 prs:
Tw each pr twice. Work lt 2 prs thro rt 2 prs.

Left side:
W thro 4 prs, tw W twice, thro 1 pr, ts with next pr.
Return with lt pr thro 1 pr, tw W twice, thro 4 prs, tw W
twice, edge st and pin. Leave.

Right side:
Work in similar manner to lt side.*

Rep from * to * for desired length. Finish with the centre
crossing of 4 prs.

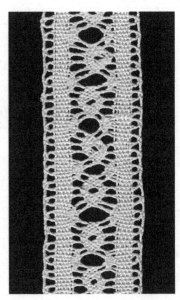

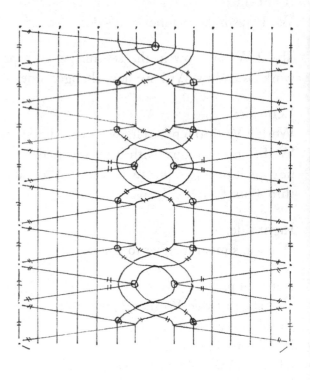

DEWDROPS
15 prs

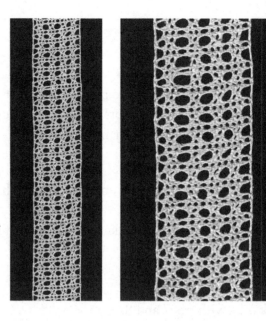

Leave edge pr and W on lt. Tw each of the 12 passive prs once.

* Divide the passive prs into 4 sets of 3 prs. Work each set thus:
Work lt pr thro the 2 prs to the rt in cls and tw.
#Work W thro each of the 12 passive prs in cls and tw, tw W once more, edge st and pin. Rep this row once more.#

Leave edge pr and W on lt. Divide the passives into 4 sets of 3 prs. Work each set thus:
Work rt pr thro the 2 prs to the lt in cls and tw.

Rep from # to #.*

Rep from * to * for desired length.

VARIATION:
The outside sets of 3 prs on the lt and rt may be worked as straight passives in cls, leaving 2 sets of dewdrops in the centre.

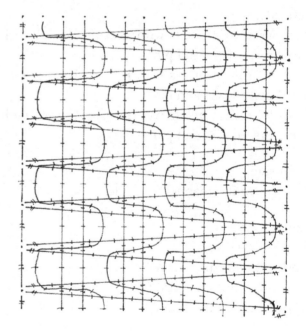

29

DOUBLE CROSS - 1
14 prs

Work in cls throughout

Work a ts with W and centre pr. Both these prs are now Ws.
Work the lt W to lt thro 5 prs, tw W twice, edge st and pin.
Work rt W to rt in similar manner. Leave.

* Centre 8 prs:
Using 2 bobbins together as one thread pass the 4 lt prs thro
the 4 rt prs in cls.
Using the bobbins singly make small plaits as follows:
Work 3 hs with prs 1 and 2.
Work 4 hs with prs 3 and 4.
Work 4 hs with prs 5 and 6.
Work 3 hs with prs 7 and 8.

Left side:
Work W thro 2 prs, ts with next pr. Return with lt pr
thro 2 prs, edge st and pin.
Work W thro 4 prs, ts with next pr. Return with lt pr
thro 4 prs, edge st and pin.
Work W thro 2 prs, ts with next pr. Return with lt pr
thro 2 prs, edge st and pin.

Right side:
Work in similar manner to lt side.

Centre 8 prs:
Work 3 hs with prs 1 and 2.
Work 4 hs with prs 3 and 4.
Work 4 hs with prs 5 and 6.
Work 3 hs with prs 7 and 8.

For the Centre 8pr Crossing:
Use 2 bobbins together as one thread and pass the 4 lt prs thro the 4 rt prs in cls.*

Repeat from * to * for desired length.

VARIATION:
Centre 8pr Crossing can be worked by using the prs singly and crossing them in hs

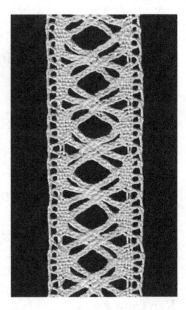

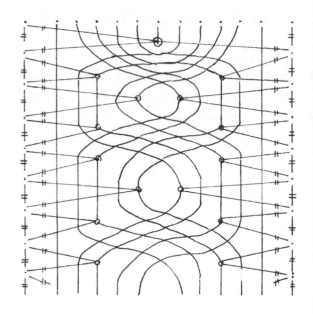

DOUBLE CROSS - 2

14 prs

Work in cls throughout.

Work a ts with W and centre pr. Both these prs are now Ws. Work lt W to lt thro 5 prs, edge st and pin.
Work rt W to rt in similar manner.

* Centre 4 prs:
Tw each pr once and work the two lt prs thro the 2 rt prs in cls and tw. Leave.

Left side:
Work W thro 2 prs, ts with 3rd pr. Return to lt with lt of these 2 prs thro 2 prs, edge st and pin.
Work W thro 3 prs to rt. Leave.
Work the 6th pr from lt thro 3 prs to lt. Leave.
Work the 7th pr from lt thro 5 prs to lt, tw twice, edge st and pin. Leave.

Right side:
Work in similar manner to left side.*

Rep from * to * for desired length.

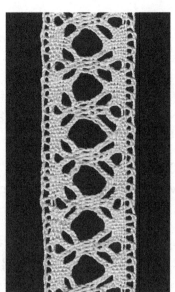

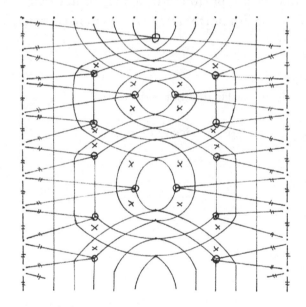

DOUBLE CROSS - 3
14 prs

Work in cls throughout.

Work a ts with W and centre pr. Both these prs are now Ws. Work lt W to lt thro 5 prs, edge st and pin. Work rt W to rt in similar manner.

* Centre 4 prs:
Tw each pr once and work the two lt prs thro the 2 rt prs in cls and tw. Leave.

Left side:
Work W thro 2 prs, ts with 3rd pr. Return to lt with lt of these 2 prs thro 2 prs, edge st and pin.
Work W thro 3 prs to rt. Leave.
Work the 6th pr from lt thro 3 prs to lt. Leave.
Work the 7th pr from lt thro 5 prs to lt, tw twice, edge st and pin. Leave.

Right side:
Work in similar manner to left side.*

Rep from * to * for desired length.

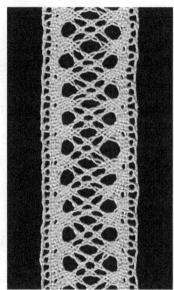

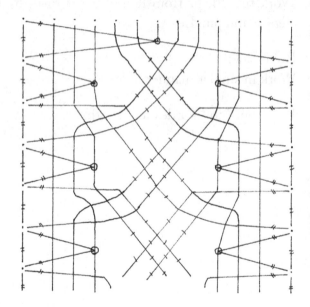

DUPLEX - 1
14 prs

Leave Ws as 7th pr from lt (there are no Ws in this braid).

Centre 8 prs:
Work 4 lt prs thro 4 rt prs in cls.
Twist all 8 prs twice each.

* Left side:
Work 4th pr from lt to the lt in cls, thro 2 prs, tw twice, work edge st and back thro 2 prs. Leave.

Work 5th pr from lt to the lt in cls, thro 3 prs, tw twice, work edge st and back thro 2 prs. Leave.

Work 6th pr from lt to the lt in cls, thro 4 prs, tw twice, work edge st and back thro 2 prs. Leave.

Work 7th pr from lt to the lt in cls, thro 5 prs, tw twice, work edge st and back thro 2 prs. Leave.

Right side:
Work in similar manner to lt side, counting prs from the rt.*

Centre 8 prs:
Tw each pr twice.
Cross 4 lt prs thro 4 rt prs in hs
Tw all 8 prs once.

Rep from * to *.#

Rep from # to # for desired length.

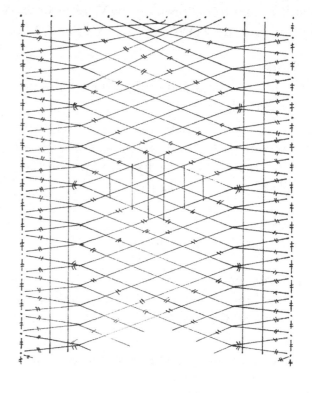

DUPLEX - 2
16 prs

Work tw with W and centre pr. Both these prs are now Ws. Work lt W to lt thro 4 prs in cls, tw W once, cls thro 2 prs, tw W twice, edge st and pin.

Work rt W to rt in similar manner. Leave.

* Centre 8 prs:
Work 4 lt prs thro 4 rt prs in cls.
Twist all 8 prs once. Leave.

Left side:
Work W thro 2 prs in cls, tw W once, work W thro 4 prs in cls and tw.

Right side:
Work W to lt thro 2 prs in cls, tw W once, work W thro 5 prs in cls and tw (Ws have changed sides). Leave.

Left side:
Take 4th pr from lt and work to the lt thro 2 prs in cls, tw it twice, edge st and pin. Work back to rt thro 2 prs in cls, tw W once, thro 2 prs in cls, ts with next pr. Take lt pr and work back to lt thro 2 prs in cls, tw W once, thro 2 prs in cls, tw W twice, edge st and pin, and work back thro 2 prs, tw W once. Leave.

Right side:
Work in similar manner to lt side.

Two centre prs:
Take the lt of these 2 prs and work it to the lt thro 4 prs in cls and tw, thro 2 prs in cls, tw W twice, edge st and pin.
Work the rt centre pr to the rt in similar manner.*

Rep from * to * for desired length.

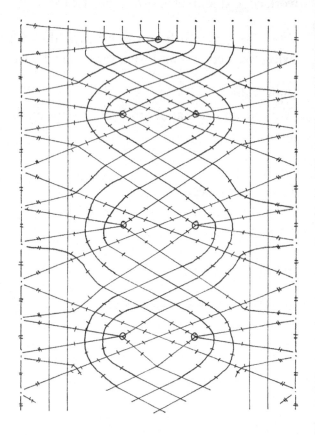

EYELET - 1
14 prs

Work ts with W and centre pr. Both these prs are now Ws.
Work lt W to lt thro 5 prs, tw twice, edge st and pin.

Work rt W to rt in similar manner.

* Left Side:
Work lt W to rt thro 3 prs, take the lt pr as new W and
work it to lt thro 2 prs, edge st and pin. Work W thro
prs, tw the next pr once and work cls, take the
pr as new W and work it to lt thro 2 prs, edge st and pin.
Leave.

Right side:
Work in similar manner to lt side.

Centre 4 prs:
Work cls and tw in the following formation:
2 lt prs, 2 rt prs, 2 centre prs.
2 lt prs, 2 rt prs, 2 centre prs.

Take 5th pr from rt, twist it once and work cls and tw
with 6th pr from rt.*

Rep from * to * for desired length.

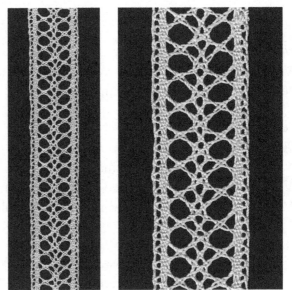

2
lt

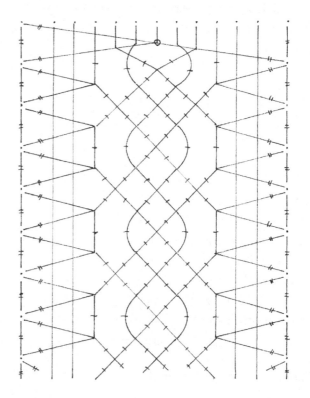

EYELET – 2
14 prs

Work ts with W and centre pr. Both these prs are now Ws.
Work lt W to lt thro 5 prs, tw W twice, edge st and pin.
Work rt W to right in similar manner.

Centre 6 prs:
Divide into 3 sets of 2 prs.
With the 2 lt prs work 3 hs (small plait made).
With the 2 prs on the rt work 3 hs (small plait made).
With the 2 prs in the centre work 4 hs (larger plait made).

* Left Side:
W thro 4 prs. Take last pr passed thro as new W and work it
to the lt thro 3 prs, tw W twice, edge st and pin. W thro 2 prs
to rt, take last pr passed thro as new W and work it to the
lt thro 1 pr, tw W twice, edge st and pin. Leave.
Take 5th and 6th prs from lt and work 3 hs (small plait
made).

Right side:
Work in similar manner to lt side.

Centre 6 prs:
2nd and 3rd prs work cls and tw.
4th and 5th prs work cls and tw.
1st and 2nd prs work small plait.
5th and 6th prs work small plait.
2 centre prs work cls and tw.
2nd and 3rd prs work cl and tw.
4th and 5th prs work cls and tw.
1st and 2nd prs work small plait.
5th and 6th prs work small plait.
2 centre prs work 4 hs (larger plait made). *

Rep from * to * for desired length.

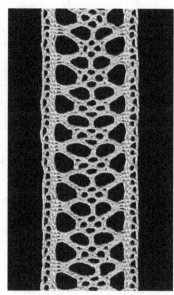
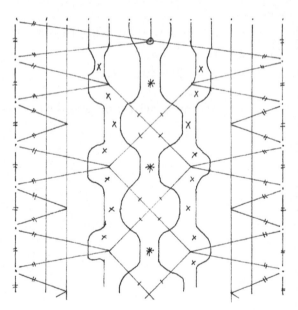

EYELET - 3
14 prs

Work ts with W and centre pr. Work lt pr to lt thro 5 prs, tw twice, edge st and pin. Leave.
Work rt pr to rt in similar manner.

Worked in cls and tw throughout, with an extra tw on edge pr

Count prs anew from the lt edge every row.

Work in prs thus:
2/3, 4/5, 6/7, 8/9, 10/11, 12/13,

* 2 out to lt, work edge, pin. Leave.
3 out to lt, work edge, pin, work back thro 1 pr. Leave.
13 out to rt, work edge, pin. Leave.
12 out to rt, work edge, pin, work back thro 1 pr. Leave.

Row 1: 5/6, 9/10.
Row 2: 4/5, 6/7, 8/9, 10/11.
Row 3: 5/6. 9/10.
Row 4: 3/4, 7/8, 11/12.
Row 5: 2/3, 4/5, 6/7, 8/9, 10/11, 12/13.*

Rep from * to * for desired length.

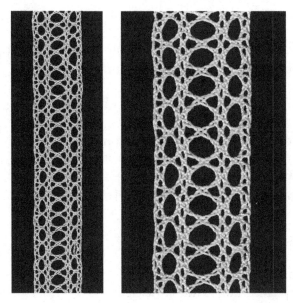

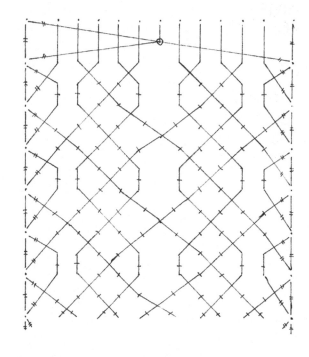

FIGURE-OF-EIGHT - 1
14 prs

Work ts with W and centre pr. Both these prs are now Ws and they work in cls throughout.

Lt W work to lt thro 5 prs, tw W twice, edge st and pin.

Work rt W in similar manner on rt side.

** Centre 6 prs:
Cross lt 3 prs thro rt 3 prs in cls. Leave.

* Left side:
W thro 4 prs, ts with next pr, return thro 4 prs, tw W twice, edge st and pin.
Rep from * once more. Leave.

Right side:
Work in similar manner to lt side.

Rep from ** for desired length, finishing with the crossover.

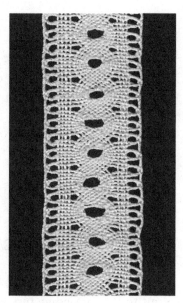

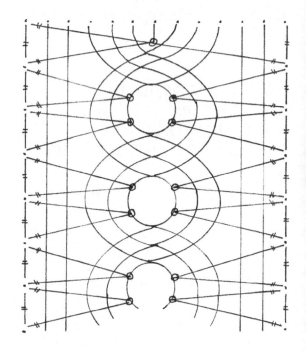

FIGURE-OF-EIGHT - 2

14 prs

Work ts with W and centre pr. Both these prs are now Ws and they work in cls throughout.

Lt W work to lt thro 5 prs, tw W twice, edge st and pin.

Work rt W in similar manner on rt side.

** Centre 6 prs:
Tw each pr once and cross lt 3 prs thro rt 3 prs with cls and one tw. Leave.

Left side:
*W thro 4 prs, ts with next pr, return thro 4 prs, tw W twice, edge st and pin.

Right side:
Work in similar manner to lt side.**

Rep from ** to ** for desired length, finishing with the crossover.

Note: In the crossover section, two twists may be used instead of one if using fine thread or if the pattern is slightly wider.

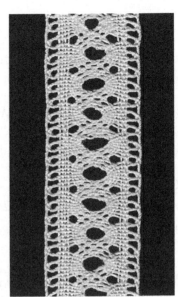

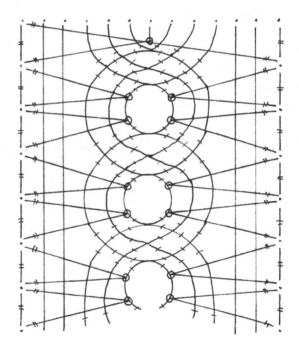

FIGURE-OF-EIGHT - 3

14 prs

Work ts with W and centre pr. Both these prs are now Ws and they work in cls throughout.

Work lt W to lt thro 5 prs, tw W twice, edge st and pin. Leave.

Work rt W in similar manner on rt side. Leave.

** Centre 4 prs:
Tw each pr twice and cross lt 2 prs thro rt 2 prs in cls and tw twice. Leave.

Left side:
* Work W thro 3 prs, tw W twice, cls and tw twice thro next 2 prs. Leave W and return to lt with last pr passed thro as new W, cls and tw twice thro 1 pr, cls thro 3 prs, tw W twice, edge st and pin.

Rep from * once more. Leave.

Right side:
Work in similar manner to lt side. Leave.**

Rep from ** to ** for desired length, finishing with the crossover.

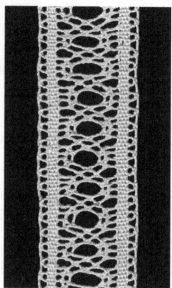

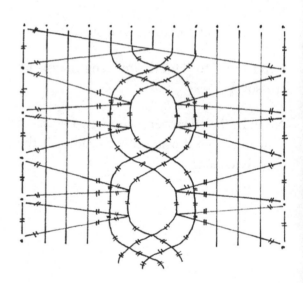

FIGURE-OF-EIGHT - 4

14 prs

Work ts with W and centre pr. Both these prs are now Ws and they work in cls throughout.

Lt W work to lt thro 5 prs, tw W twice, edge st and pin.

Work rt W in similar manner on rt side.

** Centre 6 prs:
3 lt prs: tw each pr twice.
Cross lt 3 prs thro rt 3 prs in cls.
3 rt prs: tw each pr twice. Leave.

* Left side:
W thro 2prs, tw W once, thro 2 more prs, ts with next pr.
Return with lt pr thro 2 prs, tw W once, thro 2 prs, tw W twice, edge st and pin.
Rep from * once more. Leave.

Right side:
Work in similar manner to lt side.

Rep from ** for desired length, finishing with the crossover.

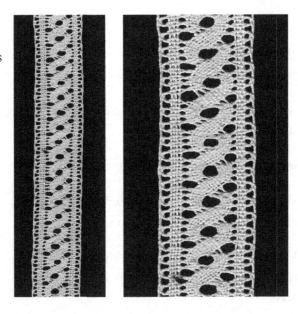

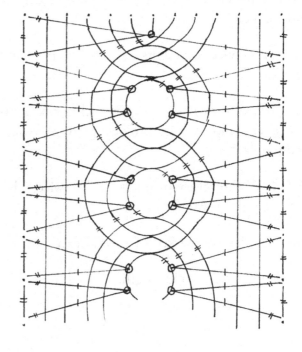

FISH - 1
13 prs

 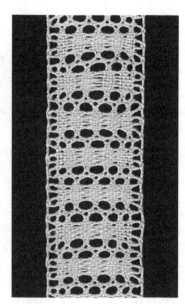

** Leave edge pr and W on lt. Tw first passive pr once. (Next 2 prs cls and tw) Rep 3 more times. Tw next pr once.

* Work W thro every pr in cls and tw, tw W once more, edge st and pin. Leave.*

(Next 2 prs cls) rep 4 more times.

Work W (thro 2 prs in cls, tw W once). Rep 4 more times, tw W once more, edge st and pin.#

(Work W thro every pr in cls, tw W twice, edge st and pin.) Rep this row once more. Then rep the row marked # to #. Leave.

(Next 2 prs cls and tw) Rep 4 more times, then rep the row marked * to *.

Tw next pr once (next 2 prs cls), rep 3 more times, tw next pr once.

Work W thro 1 pr, tw W once (thro next 2 prs, tw W once), rep 3 more times, thro next pr, tw W twice, edge st and pin.##

(Work W thro every pr in cls, tw W twice, edge st and pin.) Rep this row once more.

Then rep the row marked ## to ##. Leave.

Rep from ** for desired length.

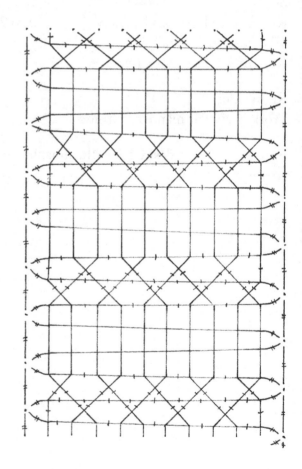

FISH - 2

13 prs

Leave edge pr and W on lt. Divide the 10 passive prs into 5 sets of 2 prs and work 1 cls with each set.

* (Work W thro 2 prs in cls, tw W twice) 5 times, edge st and pin.*
Rep from * to * once more.
Divide passives into 5 sets of 2 prs and work cls and tw with each set.
Divide the centre 8 passives into 4 sets of 2 prs and work cls with each set.
Work W in cls thro 1 pr, tw W once (W thro 2 prs, tw W once) 4 times, W thro 1 pr, tw W twice, edge st and pin.
** Work W in cls thro 10 passives, tw W twice edge st and pin.**

Rep from ** to ** once more.
Work W in cls thro 1 pr, tw W once (W thro 2 prs, tw W once) 4 times. W thro 1 pr, tw W twice, edge st and pin.
Divide centre 8 passives into 4 sets of 2 prs and work cls with each set.
Tw once the 10 passive pairs and divide them into 5 sets of 2 prs and work cls with each set.#

Rep from # to # for desired length.

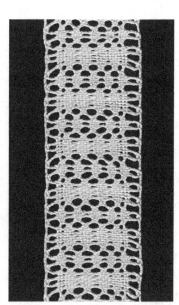

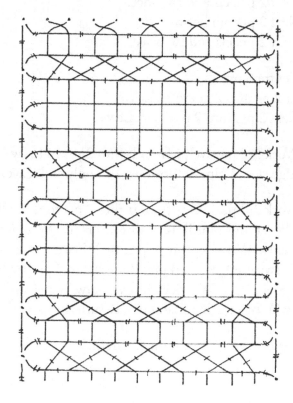

FISH - 3
16 prs

Work in cls throughout. Work W from lt to rt thro 3 prs, tw W twice, thro 4 prs, tw W twice, thro 4 more prs, tw W twice, thro 2 prs, tw W twice, edge st and pin. Return thro 2 prs. Leave.

* From the lt:
Work 2nd passive pr thro 3rd passive pr. Leave.
Work 4th and 5th passive prs thro 6th and 7th prs. Leave.
Work 8th and 9th passive prs thro 10th and 11th prs. Leave.

Centre 10 prs:
Tw each pr twice.
Lt 2 prs cls and tw twice.
Next 2 prs, pin between (make pinholes as required).
Next 2 prs, cls and tw twice.
Next 2 prs pin between.
Next 2 prs cls and tw twice.

Centre 8 prs:
Lt 2 pr thro 2 prs to rt. Leave.
Next 2 prs thro 2 prs to rt. Leave.

Work 3rd passive pr from lt thro 2 prs to lt, tw W twice, edge st and pin. Return thro 1 pr only and leave.

Work 3rd passive pr from rt thro 2 prs to rt, tw W twice, edge st and pin. Return thro 2 prs, tw W twice, thro 4 prs, tw W twice, thro 4 prs, tw W twice, thro 3 prs, tw W twice, edge st and pin. Return thro 3 prs, tw W twice, thro 4 prs, tw W twice, thro 4 prs, tw W twice, thro 2 prs, tw W twice, edge st and pin. Return thro 2 prs. Leave.*

Rep from * to * for desired length.

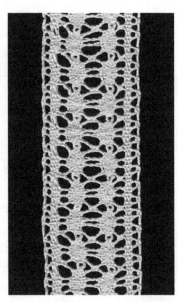

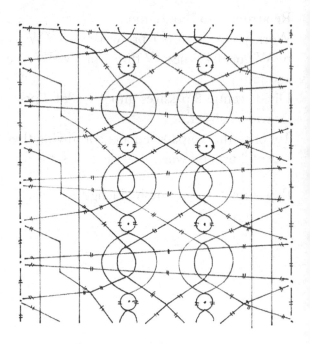

FISHES - with 2 or 4 horizontals
13 prs

Ws work in cls throughout.

The fishes:
*Work W thro 2 prs, tw W once. Rep from * to end of row, tw W once more, edge st and pin.

For 2 horizontals, rep this row once more.

For 4 horizontals, rep the row three more times.

The lattice work:
Leave W with the edge pr.

* Work cls and tw once with next 2 prs. Leave.
Rep from * to end of row, leaving the other edge pr unworked.
Work the W thro next pr in cls and tw. Leave.

** Work the next 2 prs in cls and tw. Leave.
Rep from ** to end of row, including the edge pr, which should be twisted twice and pin up under 2 prs.
Work the inside pr of these last 2 prs with the next pr in cls. Leave.

*** Work the next 2 prs in cls (no tw). Leave.

Rep from *** to last 2 prs.

Work edge st and pin with these last 2 prs.

Rep from # for desired length.

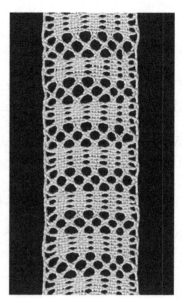

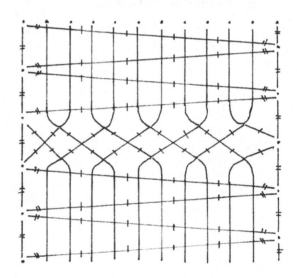

FRET

15 prs

Twist 10 centre passive prs once.

Divide centre passive prs into 5 sets of 2 prs and work cls and tw with each set (small plait made).

* Work W thro 2 prs in cls, tw W once, thro 8 prs in half-stitch, thro 2 prs in cls, tw W twice, edge st and pin.*

Rep from * to * twice more. Leave.

Divide centre passive prs into 5 sets of 2 prs and work cls and tw with each set.

Rep from * to * five times. #

Rep from # to # for desired length.

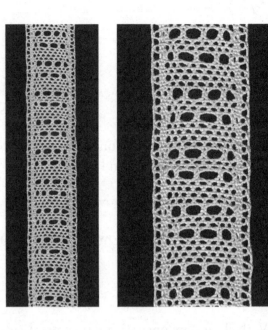

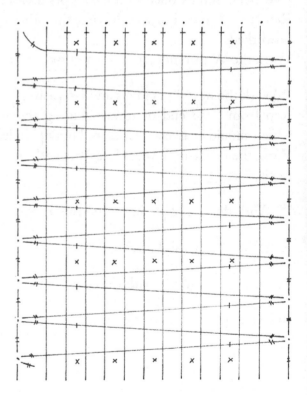

GRENADES
15 prs

Work 2 rows of cls with edge st.

* Divide the 12 passive prs into 3 sets of 4 prs.
Work each set as follows:
Cls with lt 2 prs.
Cls with rt 2 prs.
Using each pr as one thread work cls with the 4 prs.
Using the threads singly again:
Cls with lt 2 prs.
Cls with rt 2 prs.

When each of the 3 sets has been worked in this way, continue as follows:

(Work W thro each passive pr in cls and tw once, extra tw before edge st and pin.) Rep this row 3 more times, but in the last row do not twist the passive prs. *

Rep from * to * for desired length, finishing with the crossing of each set.

Note: If preferred, 1 grenade may be worked in the centre, the passive prs on each side being worked in cls.

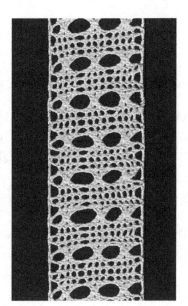

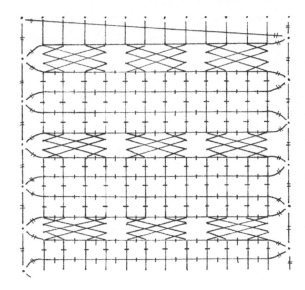

HALOED FISH

13 prs

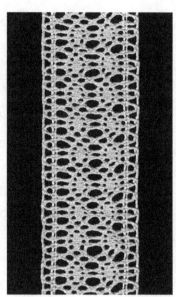

The fishes:

Work cls with 5th and 6th prs and with the 9th and 10th prs.

* Work W in cls thro 1 pr, tw W once, cls and tw thro 1 pr, cls thro 2 prs, tw W once, cls and tw thro 2 prs, cls thro 2 prs, tw W once, cls and tw thro 1 pr, cls thro 1 pr, tw W twice, edge st and pin.
Rep from * once more.

Work W thro 1 pr, tw W. Leave these 2 prs and edge pr. Work cls and tw with 5th and 6th prs and with 9th and 10th prs.

Lattice work:
With 4 prs from first fish:
Cls and tw with 2 lt prs and same with the rt 2 prs. Leave. With 4 prs from second fish: Work in similar manner to first fish. Leave.

W and next pr: cls and tw. Leave. (Take the next 2 prs: cls and tw.) Rep twice more, leave. Next pr thro 1 pr in cls, tw twice, edge st and pin. Return thro 1 pr, tw and work cls and tw thro next pr. Leave. (Take next 2 prs: cls and tw.) Rep twice more, leave. Next pr thro 1 pr in cls, tw twice, edge st and pin. Leave.

Rep from # for desired length, finishing with the lattice work.

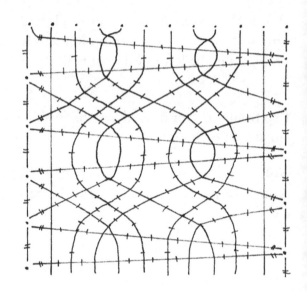

HOLE - 1 AND 2
14 prs

HOLE – 1

To be worked in cls braid.

Leave W at edge.

Work hs with 5th and 6th passive prs. Work W thro and make ts with W and the nearest of these two prs. W returns thro 4 prs, tw W twice, edge st and pin. Leave.

Other side:
Take remaining pr from hs as W and work thro 5 prs, tw W twice, edge st and pin. Return thro 5 prs, tw W and next pr once and cross centre bobbins lt over rt (a reverse hs. Leave these two prs to become passives.

Continue braid with the original W.

HOLE - 2

This gives a smaller hole than Hole 1.

To be worked in cls braid.

Work W to where the hole is required, usually in the centre of the braid, tw W and last pr passed thro 3 times, work W thro next pr and tw this pr 3 times but not the W. Work W to end of row.

In the next row, the W only is twisted 3 times between the two twisted passive prs.

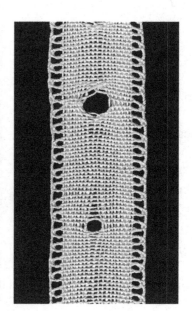

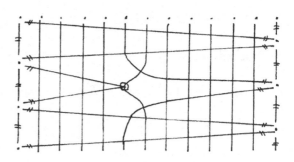

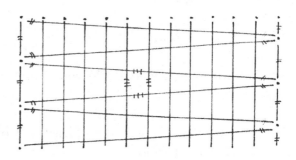

HOLE - 3 AND 4
13 prs

HOLE - 3

To be worked in cls braid.

Leave W at edge.

Centre 4 passive prs:
Centre 2 prs: tw 3 times
Lt 2 prs cls
Rt 2 prs cls
Centre 2 prs: tw 3 times

Continue braid with the original W.

HOLE - 4

This is a larger hole than Hole 3

To be worked in cls braid

Work W thro 5prs, tw W twice, W thro 5 more prs, edge st and pin. Leave.

Centre 4 prs:
Centre 2 prs tw twice each
Work 2 lt prs in cls
Work 2 rt prs in cls
Centre 2 prs tw twice each

Work W thro 5 prs, tw W twice, W thro 5 more prs, edge st and pin. Leave.

Continue with plain cls braid for at least four or five rows before working another hole.

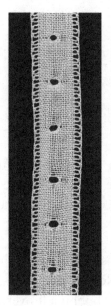
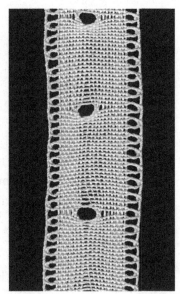

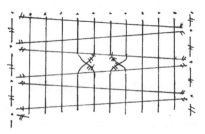

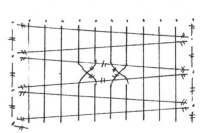

HOOKED - 1

12 prs

No W required (leave as a passive).

Centre 8 prs:
Tw each pr twice and divide into 2 sets of 4 prs. Work each set as follows:
2 centre prs cls and tw twice.
2 lt prs cls and tw twice.
2 rt prs cls and tw twice.
2 centre prs cls and tw twice.

* Left side:
Work 3rd pr from lt to the lt thro 1 pr, cls and tw W twice and passive once, edge st and pin. (Return thro inner edge pr and next pr, cls and tw. Return to lt with last pr passed thro and work cls and tw thro 1pr, tw W once more, edge st and pin.) Rep twice more. Return thro inner edge pr, cls and tw, W once more.

Right side:
Work in similar manner to lt side.

Centre spider:
Using centre 4 prs, work as follows:
2 centre prs cls and tw twice.
2 lt prs cls and tw twice.
2 rt prs cls and tw twice.
2 centre prs cls and tw twice.
2 lt prs cls and tw twice.
2 rt prs cls and tw twice.
2 centre prs cls and tw twice.

Left spider:
With the 2 lt prs from centre spider and the next 2 prs to the lt, work another spider.

Right spider:
With the 2 rt prs from the centre spider and the next 2 prs to the rt, work another spider.*

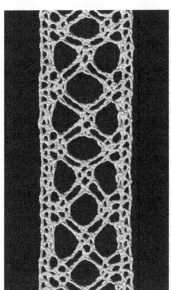

51

Rep from * to * for desired length, finishing with half-made lt and rt spiders.

Note: A variation on this design may be made giving only one twist instead of two on all the crossings. This would be suitable for a narrower braid.

HOOKED - 2
12 prs

Work in cls and tw twice throughout. W left as a passive.

Centre 8 prs:
Divide into 2 sets of 4 prs.
Work each set: lt 2 prs thro rt 2 prs.

* Spider with centre 4 prs:
Lt 2 pr thro rt 2 prs.
Work 2 lt prs.
Work 2 rt prs.
Work 2 centre prs.

Left side:
3rd pr from lt thro 2 prs to lt. Pin under 2 prs and close pin with 2 inside prs.
4th pr from lt thro 3 prs to lt. Pin under 2 prs and close pin with 2 inside prs.
Work lt spider with 3rd, 4th, 5th and 6th prs from lt.

Right side:
Work in similar manner to lt side.*

Rep from * to * for desired length.

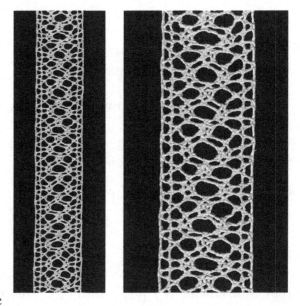

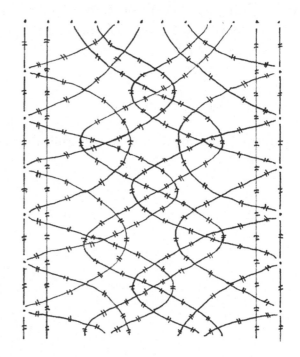

HORSESHOES
14 prs

Work ts with W and centre pr. Both these prs are now Ws and they work in cls throughout.

Work lt W to lt, thro 5 prs, tw W twice, edge st and pin. Leave.

Work rt W to rt in similar manner. Leave.

* Centre 6 prs tw each once and cross lt 3 prs thro rt 3 prs in cls.

Left side:
Work W thro 2 prs, tw W once, thro 2 more prs, ts with next pr (put aside remaining 7 prs), return thro 2 prs, tw W once, thro 2 prs, tw W twice, edge st and pin.
W thro 2 prs in cls, tw W once, thro 1 more pr, ts with next pr, return thro 1 pr, tw W once, thro 2 prs, tw W twice, edge st and pin.

Right side:
Work in similar manner to lt side.*

Rep from * to * for desired length, finishing with the crossover.

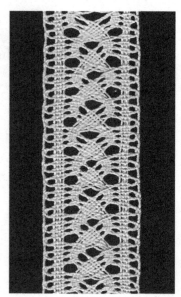

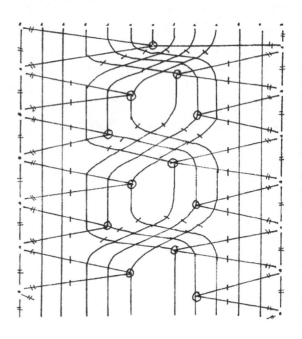

ICONIC
14 prs

Work ts with W and centre pr. Both these prs are now Ws.
Work lt W to lt thro 5 prs, edge st and pin.
Work rt W to rt in similar manner.

* Work lt W thro 5 prs to rt, tw W once.
Work rt W thro 5 prs to lt, tw W once.
Work the two Ws together with cls and tw. Work the lt
pr to lt thro 5 prs, edge st and pin and work the rt pr to rt
thro 5 prs, edge st and pin.*

Rep from * to * once more.

Left side:
Work W thro 5 prs to rt, tw W twice. Leave.
Take last pr passed thro as new W and work it to lt
thro 4 prs, edge st and pin. Work W back thro 4 prs
(no twist). Leave.

Right side:
Work in similar manner to lt side.

Two centre prs:
Work together with cls and tw twice. Both these prs
are Ws.

Work lt W to lt thro 5 prs, tw W twice, edge st and
pin.
Work rt W to rt in similar manner.#

Rep from # to # for desired length.

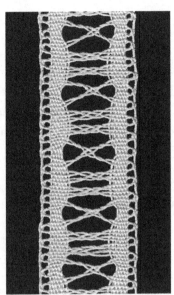

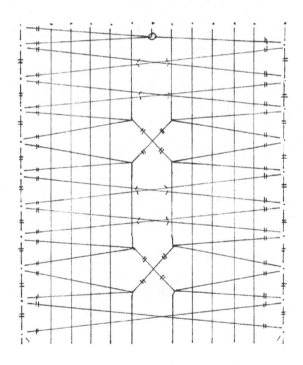

ITALIAN FISH - 1
13 prs

Work W thro one passive pr in cls, tw W once.

** The lattice work:
* Cross prs 4 and 5 thro prs 6 and 7 in cls.
Cross prs 8 and 9 thro prs 10 and 11 in cls.*

Tw these 8 prs once.

Cross the centre 4 prs in cls and tw.

Work pr 4 thro the W in cls and tw, then thro 1 pr, tw twice, edge st and pin. Return thro 1 pr, tw once. Leave.

Pr 5 also works thro to edge: thro 2 prs in cls and tw, thro 1 pr in cls, tw twice, edge st and pin.

Return thro 1 pr, tw once. This pr will become the W for the next set of fishes.

Work the opposite edge in a similar manner, using pr 11 first and then pr 10.

Rep from * to * once.

The fishes:
(W thro 2 prs, tw W once) 4 times, W thro 1 pr, tw W twice, edge st and pin. Return thro 1 pr, tw W once.

Rep from # three more times.

Rep from ** for desired length, finishing with the lattice work.

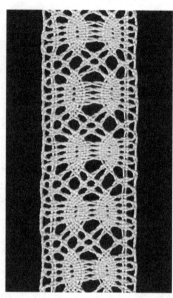

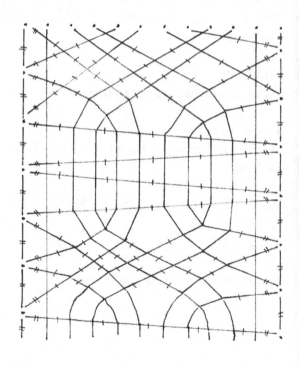

ITALIAN FISH - 2
17 prs

From lt, work W thro 1 pr cls and tw, **(thro 2 prs in cls, tw W twice) six times, thro 1 pr, tw W twice, edge st and pin.
Work W back to lt keeping twists in same places, work edge st and pin.
Work W to rt thro 1 pr in cls and tw. Leave.
Put aside 3 prs on lt and 2 prs on rt.
Work remaining 12 prs in groups of 2 prs in cls and tw.
Then cross the centre 10 prs in groups of 2 prs in cls and tw.
Work 4th pr from lt to lt in cls and tw, edge st and pin and back thro 1 pr. Leave.
Work 3rd pr from rt to rt edge, cls and tw, pin, and back thro 1 pr cls and tw. Leave.
Put aside 3 prs on lt and 2 prs on rt.
Work remaining 12 prs in 3 sets of 4 prs:

Each set of 4:
Cls 2 lt prs.
Cls 2 rt prs.
Cls centre prs.
Cls 2 lt prs, tw lt pr only.
Cls 2 rt prs, tw rt pr only.
* Work 4th pr from lt to the lt edge cls and tw, pin and back thro 1 pr.
Cross prs 7 and 8 cls and tw.
Cross prs 11 and 12 cls and tw.
Work 3rd pr from rt to the rt edge cls and tw, pin and back thro 1 pr.*
Put aside 3 prs on lt and 2 prs on rt.

Work remaining 12 prs in 3 sets of 4 prs:
Cls 2 lt prs.
Cls 2 rt prs.
Cls 2 centre prs.
Cls 2 lt prs.
Cls 2 rt prs.
Cls 2 centre prs.
Tw all 4 prs once.

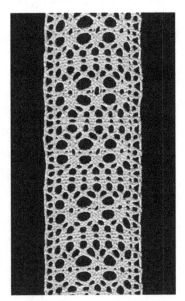

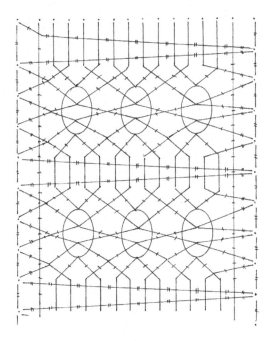

Rep from * to * once.

Put aside 3 prs on lt and 2 prs on rt.
Work remaining 2 prs in groups of 2 prs in cls and tw. **

Take Ws (3rd pr from lt) and repeat from ** to ** for desired length.

ITALIAN SPIDER
15 prs

W on rt of braid.

Work W in cls thro 7 passive prs and ts with next pr. Both these prs are now Ws. Both prs work out to each edge: the lt W to the lt and the rt W to the rt. At each edge, pin under 2 prs and close pin with inside pr in cls and tw. Leave.

Centre 9 passive prs:
Work each of the 3 lt prs in turn thro the rt 6 prs in cls.
Tw once the lt 3 prs and the rt 3 prs.
Tw 3 times the centre 3 prs.

Set aside the 9 prs on rt.

Net ground:
Work in cls and tw with the lt 6 prs.
Work the 3rd pr from lt thro 3 prs to rt.
Work the (new) 3rd pr from lt to the lt thro 2 edge prs, pin, close the pin with the inner edge pr and work thro 2 more prs to the rt.
Work the (new) 3rd pr from the lt to the lt, thro 2 edge prs, pin, close the pin with the inner edge pr and work thro 1 more pr to the rt.
Work the (new) 3rd pr from lt to the lt, thro 2 edge prs, pin, close the pin with the inner edge pr.

Set aside these 6 prs and the 3 centre prs (which are twisted 3 times). Work the net ground with the rt 6 prs in similar manner to lt side.

Work lt spider in cls:
Prs 4, 5 and 6 from lt, work thro the centre 3 prs.
Intersect the spider by working the 3rd pr from lt edge thro all these 6 prs, tw once, cls and tw thro the next pr to the rt. The lt of these two returns to lt thro the 6 prs, tw once, cls and tw thro the 2 edge prs, pin and close the pin. Leave.

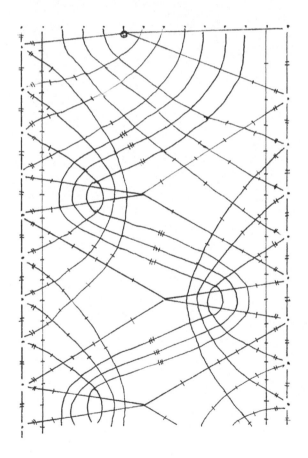

Complete the spider by working the 3 lt prs thro the 3 rt prs, tw lt 3 prs once and rt 3 prs three times.

Work the 6th pr from rt, which intersected the spider, in cls and tw thro 4 prs to rt, edge st and pin, close pin. Leave.

Work the net ground on the lt with the lt 6 prs. Work spider on rt in similar manner to lt spider, using centre 3 prs which have been twisted 3 times and 3 prs to the rt. Work the net ground on the rt with the rt 6 prs.

Continue in this manner so that the order of working is:
Spider on lt.
Net ground on lt.
Spider on rt.
Net ground on rt.

Finish with spider on rt and net ground on both sides, then work 3 lt passive prs thro 6 prs on rt. Work Ws from both sides to centre and make a ts, 1 pr remaining as W and 1 pr becoming a passive.

Turn diagram upside down to see the method of finishing.

JINKS
14 prs

Work ts with W and centre pr. Both these prs are now Ws and they work in cls throughout.

Work lt W thro 5 prs to lt, tw W twice, edge st and pin. Leave.

Work rt W to rt in similar manner. Leave.

Centre 2 prs:

Cls and tw.

* Work lt W thro 5 prs to centre.

Work rt W thro 6 prs. The Ws have now changed sides.

Left side:
Work lt W thro 5 prs to lt, tw W twice, edge st and pin.
Work W thro 3 prs, ts with next pr, return thro 3 prs, tw W twice, edge st and pin. Leave.

Right side:
Work in similar manner to lt side. Leave.

Centre 4 prs:
Tw each pr once.
Cross lt 2 prs thro rt 2 prs in cls and tw once.*

Rep from * to * for desired length.

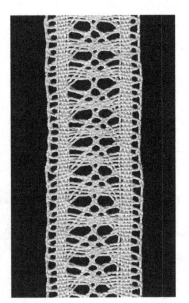

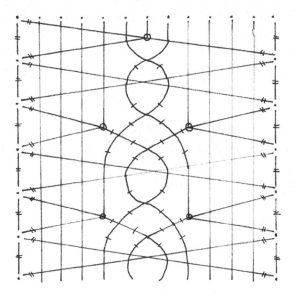

KISSES
13 prs

Work 2 rows in cls with edge st.

W works in cls throughout.

Leave W and edge pr.

Centre 4 prs:

Cross 2 lt prs thro 2 rt prs in cls (no tw).

Tw once each of the 2 prs on the lt and 2 prs on the rt of the centre 4 prs.

Work W thro 1 pr, tw W once, thro 2 prs, tw once W and last 2 prs passed thro, W thro 2 prs, tw W once, thro 2 prs, tw W once, thro 2 prs, tw once W and last 2 prs passed thro, W thro 1 pr, tw W twice, edge st and pin.

* Work W thro 1 pr, (tw W once, W thro 2 prs) 4 times, tw W once, thro 1 pr, tw W twice, edge st and pin.*

Centre 8 prs:
Divide into 2 groups of 4 prs.
Each group: lt pr tw once, 2 centre prs cls, rt pr tw once.

Rep from * to * twice. #

To repeat the whole pattern work from # to #.

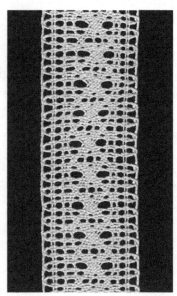

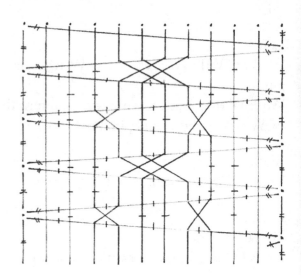

LADDER - 1

14 prs

Work in cls throughout.

Work a ts with W and centre passive pr. Both these prs are now Ws.

Work lt W to lt thro 5 prs, edge st and pin. Work rt W to rt in similar manner.

* Left side:
W thro 2 prs, tw W twice, thro 3 prs, tw W once. Leave.

Right side:
Work in similar manner to lt side.

Work the two Ws together in cls and tw. (The Ws have now changed sides.)

Left side:
W thro 3 prs, tw W twice, thro 2 prs, edge st and pin.

Right side:
Work in similar manner to lt side.*

Rep from * to * for desired length.

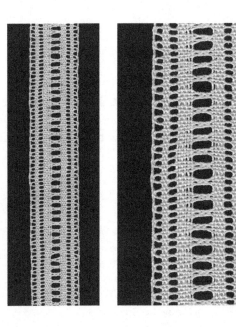

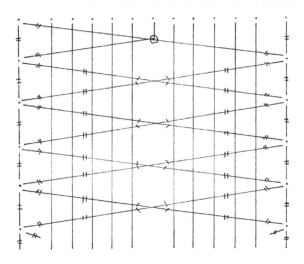

LADDER - 2
14 prs

Work in cls throughout.

Work ts with W and centre pr. Both these prs are now Ws.

* Work lt W to lt thro 5 prs, tw twice, edge st and pin.

Work rt W to rt in similar manner.

10 passive prs:

Tw each pr twice.

Work lt W to rt thro 5 prs.
Work rt W to lt thro 5 prs.

Tw the two Ws once and work cls and tw.*

Rep from * to *.

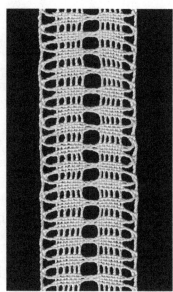

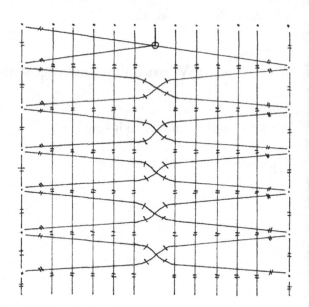

LADDER - 3
14 prs

Work ts with W and centre pr. Both these prs are now Ws.
Work lt W to lt thro 5 prs in cls, tw twice, edge st and pin.
Work rt W to rt in similar manner.

* Left side:
Work W thro 3 prs in cls, tw W once, cls and tw thro 2
prs. Leave.

Right side:
Work in similar manner to lt side.

Centre 2 prs:
Cls and tw. (Ws have changed sides)

Left side:
Work W thro 2 prs in cls and tw, thro 3 prs in cls, tw
W twice, edge st and pin.

Right side:
Work in similar manner to lt side.*

Rep from * to * for desired length.

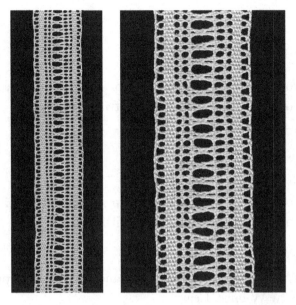

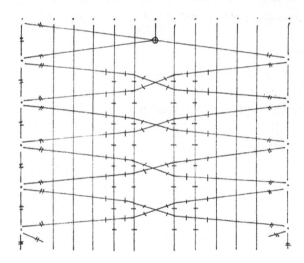

LADDER - 4

14 prs

Work in cls throughout.

Work a ts with W and centre pr. Both these prs are now Ws. Work lt W to lt thro 5 prs, tw twice, edge st and pin. Work rt W to rt in similar manner.

* Centre 2 prs:
Cls and tw.
Work the lt pr to the lt thro 2 prs and tw it once.
Work the rt pr to the rt in similar manner.

Left side:
W thro 2 prs, tw W once, cls and tw thro next pr, cls thro 2 prs tw W once. Leave.
Take the 4th pr from lt, which has one twist, and work it to the lt thro 2 prs, tw twice, edge st and pin.

Right side:
Work in similar manner to lt side.*

Rep from * to * for desired length.

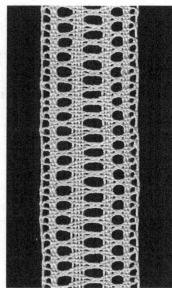

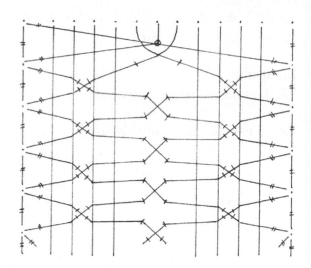

LADDER - 5

14 prs

Work ts with W and centre pr. Both these prs are now Ws.
Work lt W to lt thro 5 prs, tw W twice, edge st and pin.
Work rt W to rt in similar manner. Leave.

Counting from lt, tw prs 5, 6, 9 and 10 once.

* Left side:
Work W thro 2 prs in cls, tw W once, thro 2 prs in half-stitch, thro 1 pr in cls, tw W once. Leave.

Right side:
Work in similar manner to lt side.

Two Ws in the centre:
Cls and tw. (Ws have changed sides.)

Left side:
Work W thro 1 pr in cls, tw W once, thro 2 prs in half-stitch, thro 2 prs in cls, tw W twice, edge st and pin.

Right side:
Work in a similar manner.*

Rep from * to * for desired length.

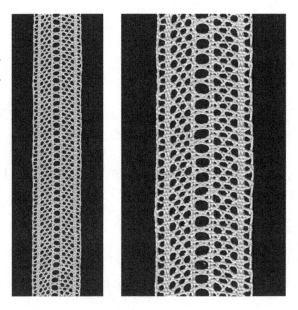

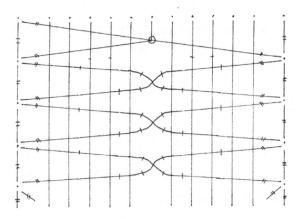

LATTICE - 1
13 prs

 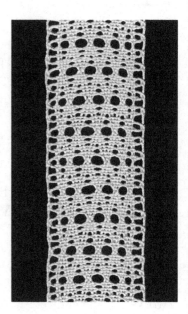

* Leave edge pr and W on lt.

(Take next 2 passive prs and work cls. Leave.) Rep 5 times. Leave the rt edge pr unworked.

(Work W thro 2 prs in cls, tw W once) Rep 5 times. Tw W once more, edge st and pin.

Rep from # to # once more.

** Work W thro 1 pr in cls, tw W once. (W thro 2 prs, tw W once) Rep 4 times. W thro 1 pr, tw W twice, edge st and pin.**

Rep from ** to ** once more.

Leave edge pr and W on lt. Tw 1st passive pr once. (Take next 2 passive prs and work cls) Rep 4 times. Tw last passive pr once.

Rep from ** to ** twice.

Rep from # to # twice.*

Rep from * to * for desired length, finishing with the crossing of the passive prs.

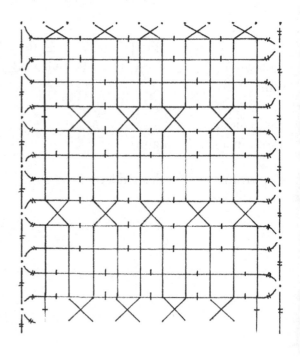

LATTICE - 2
15 prs

* Leave edge pr and W on lt. Divide centre 8 passive prs into 2 sets of 4 prs.

With each set work a 4-pr crossing thus:

Use 2 bobbins as 1 thread and work 1 cls.

Work W in cls thro 2 prs, tw W twice. (W thro 4 prs, tw W twice) Rep 2 times. W thro 2 prs, tw W twice, edge st and pin.#

Rep from # to # twice more.

** (Work W in cls thro 4 prs, tw W twice) Rep 3 times. Edge st and pin.**

Rep from ** to ** twice more.

Leave edge pr and W on lt. Divide passive prs into 3 sets of 4 prs. With each set work a 4-pr crossing (as above).

Rep from ** to ** 3 times.

Rep from # to # 3 times.

Rep from * to * for desired length, finishing with sets of 4-pr crossings.

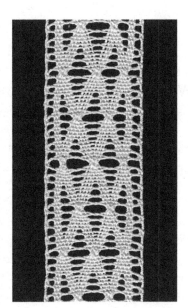
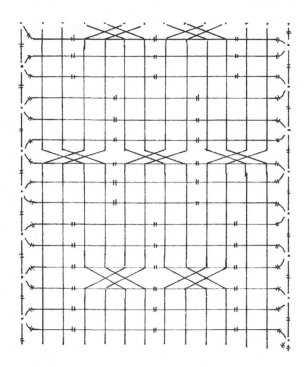

LATTICE - 3
15 prs

 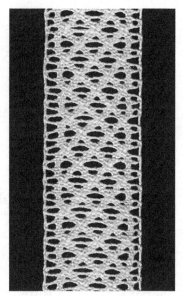

* Leave edge pr and W on lt. Divide the 12 passive prs into 3 sets of 4 prs.
With each set work a 4-pr crossing thus:
Use 2 bobbins as 1 thread and work 1 cls.

(Work W in cls thro 2 prs, tw W twice) Rep 5 more times. Edge st and pin.#

Rep from # to # once more.

Leave edge pr and W.

Work cls with first 2 passive prs. Divide next 8 passive prs into 2 sets of 4 prs and work a 4-pr crossing with each set, as above. Work cls with last 2 passive prs.

** (Work W in cls thro 2 prs, tw W twice) Rep 5 more times. Edge st and pin.**

Rep from ** to ** once more.*

Rep from * to * for desired length, finishing with a 4-pr crossing.

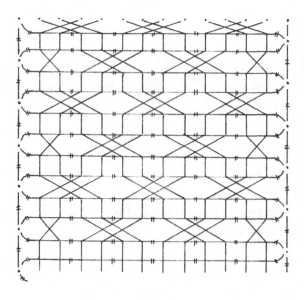

LAZY-TONGS
14 prs

Work in cls throughout.
Work ts with W and centre pr. Both these prs are now Ws.

Work lt W thro 5 prs to lt, tw W twice, edge st and pin, work back thro one pr. Leave.
Work rt side in similar manner.

* Centre 8 prs:
Tw each pr twice.
Cross 4 lt prs thro 4 rt prs.
Tw each pr twice.

Left side:
Work first pr (from centre 8 prs) thro 2 prs to lt (no tw). Leave.

Work 2nd pr thro 3 prs to lt, tw twice, edge st and pin, work back thro one pr. Leave.

Work 3rd pr thro 4 prs to lt. Leave.

Work 4th pr thro 5 prs to lt, tw twice, edge st and pin, work back thro 1 pr. Leave.

Right side:
Work in similar manner to lt side.*

Rep from * to * for desired length.

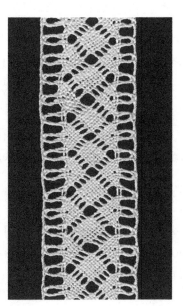

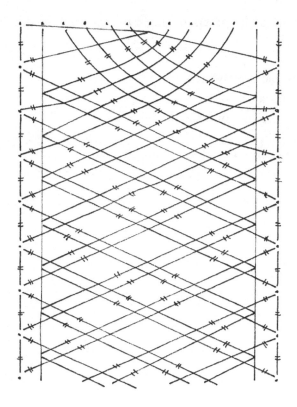

LITTLE SPIDERS
14 prs

Ts with W and centre pr. Both prs work out to their respective edges, close the pin and leave as the second passive.

Centre 8 prs:
Lt 4 prs: pass the lt 2 prs thro the rt 2 prs in cls.
Work rt 4 prs in similar manner.

* Tw 8 prs twice.
Lt 2 prs: work the first pr thro 2 prs to the lt in cls, tw twice, edge st, pin, return thro 2 prs. Leave.
Work the second pr thro 3 prs to the lt in cls, tw twice, edge st, pin, return thro 2 prs.
Rt 2 prs (of the 8 centre prs) work in similar manner to the rt.

Centre 4 prs:
Work a cls spider, making a ts (optional) in the centre.

Centre 8 prs:
Tw each pr twice.
Work a cls spider with lt 4 prs.
Work a cls spider with rt 4 prs.

Rep from * for desired length.

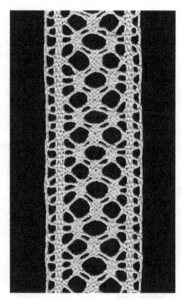

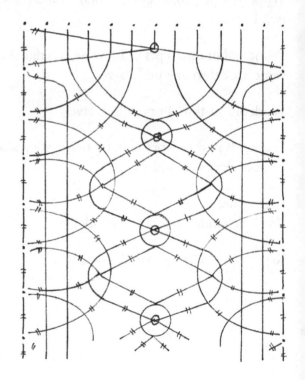

LOTUS - 1
15 prs

* Leave edge pr and W on lt. Work first 2 passive prs in cls. Leave. Divide the next 8 prs into 2 sets of 4 prs and work a 4-pr crossing with each set thus:
Using 2 bobbins as one thread, work 1 cls.
Then using the bobbins singly, work 1 cls with 2 lt prs and 1 cls with 2 rt prs.
Work last 2 passive prs in cls. Leave.

Divide all the passives into 3 sets of 4 prs and with each set, work a 4-pr crossing thus:

Using 2 bobbins as 1 thread, work 1 cls.

(Work W in cls thro 4 prs, tw W twice) Rep twice more. Edge st and pin.#

Rep from # to # twice more.

** Work W in cls thro 2 prs, tw W twice, W thro 4 prs, tw W twice, W thro 4 more prs, tw W twice, W thro 2 prs, tw W twice, edge st and pin.**

Rep from ** to ** twice more.*

Rep from * to * for desired length, finishing with the 4-pr crossings.

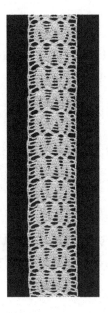

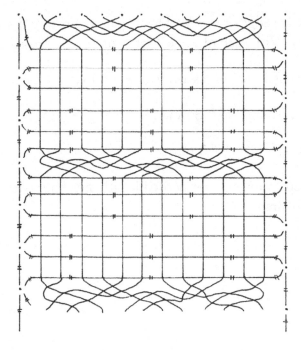

LOTUS - 2
15 prs

* Leave edge pr and W on lt. Divide the centre 8 passives prs into 2 sets of 4 prs. With each of these 2 sets work a 4-pr crossing thus:
Using 2 bobbins as 1 thread work 1 cls.

(Work W thro 4 prs in cls, tw W twice) Rep 3 times, edge st and pin.

Rep from # to # twice more.

** Work W thro 2 prs in cls, tw W twice (work W thro 4 prs in cls, tw W twice) rep once more, W thro 2 prs, tw W twice, edge st and pin.**

Rep from ** to ** twice more.

Leave edge pr and W. Divide passive prs into 3 sets of 4 prs. With each of these 3 sets work a 4-pr crossing thus:

Using 2 bobbins as 1 thread, work 1 cls.

Rep from ** to ** 3 times.

Rep from # to # 3 times.

Rep from * to * for desired length, finishing with a 4-pr crossing.

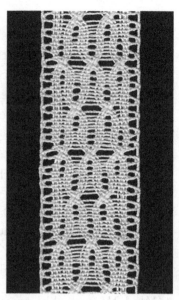

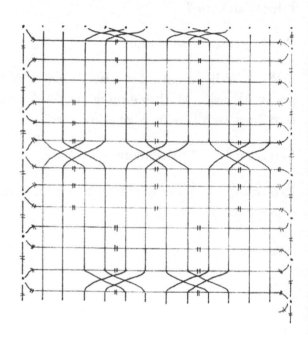

LOTUS - 3
15 prs

Work 2 rows of cls with edge st.

* Leave edge pr and W on lt. Divide passive prs into 3 sets of 4 prs. With each set work a 4-pr crossing thus:
Using 2 bobbins as 1 thread work 1 cls.

Work W thro 2 prs in cls, tw W once, rep to end of row, tw W once more, edge st and pin.

Rep from # to # 5 more times.*

Rep from * to * for desired length.

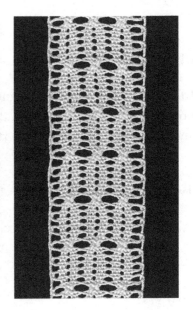

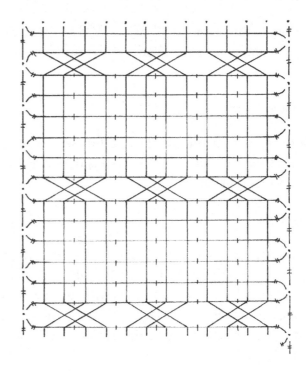

MALTESE SPOT & MAY BUD
14 prs

MALTESE SPOT

In cls braid, make ts with W and centre pr. Both these prs are now Ws. Work the lt W to lt, thro 5 prs, tw W twice, edge st and pin. Leave. Work rt W to rt in similar manner.

Centre 2 prs:
Tw twice, cls.

Work lt W thro 4 prs, tw twice, cls thro next pr. Leave.

Work rt W thro 4 prs, tw twice, cls thro next pr.

Two Ws:
Cls. Ws have now changed sides.

Lt W cls thro 1 pr, tw W twice, W thro 4 prs, tw twice, edge st and pin. Leave. Work rt W in similar manner.

Centre 2 prs:
Cls and tw twice.

Both Ws to centre and make ts. Of these two prs, the one nearest the next hole to be worked is the W. The other pr remains as a passive.

MAY BUD

In cls braid, make ts with W and centre pr. Both these prs are now Ws. Work lt W thro 5 prs to lt, tw W twice, edge st and pin. Work W thro 4 prs, ts with next pr, return thro 4 prs, tw W twice, edge st and pin. Work W thro 2 prs, ts with next pr, return thro 2 prs, tw W twice, edge st and pin. Leave.

Work rt W to rt in similar manner.

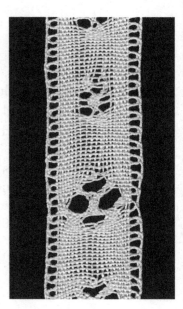
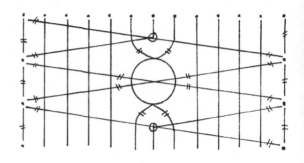
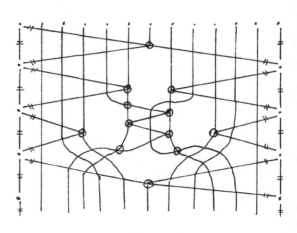

Centre 4 prs:

Work cls with 2 rt prs.

Work ts with 2 lt prs. Taking the rt of these 2 prs, work backwards and forwards 4 times in cls and ts at each end. Finish with ts on lt. Leave.

Ts with 2 rt prs.

Cross the 2 lt prs thro the 2 prs on the lt of them in cls.

Work the 2 rt prs (of the original centre 4 prs) to the rt in a similar manner.

Work both Ws to centre and work ts. Of these two prs, the one nearest the next hole to be worked is the W. The other pr remains as a passive.

MEANDER-IN-BRAID - 1
14 prs

Work 1 row of cls, make edge st and pin with last pr, tw both prs twice. Leave.

Make hs with 7th and 8th passive prs. Leave.

#* Work W in cls thro 3 prs, tw W twice, thro 3 more prs, and make ts with next pr (put aside the remaining 5 prs), return with W thro 3 prs, tw W twice, thro 3 more prs, tw W twice and make edge st and pin.

Rep from * once more.

Leave edge pr, W and 3 passive prs. #

Other side:

Take remaining pr from hs as W, work cls thro 3 prs, tw W twice, edge st and pin, tw both prs twice.

Rep from # to # as on first side.

Each side continues to work alternately.

To change to plain braid, work W thro 3 passive prs and make a reverse hs with W and next pr. To see this more clearly, turn diagram upside down and note where passives 7 and 8 opened the braid.

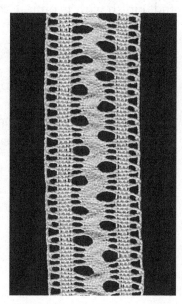

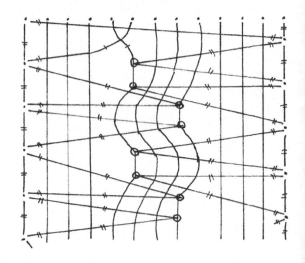

MEANDER-IN-BRAID - 2
13 prs

* W cls thro 2 prs, tw W once, cls and tw thro next pr, cls thro 4 prs, ts with next pr. Return thro 4 prs, tw W once, cls and tw thro next pr, cls thro 2 prs, tw W twice, edge st and pin.*

W cls thro 2 prs, tw W once, cls and tw thro next pr, cls thro 4 prs, tw W and next pr once and make cls and tw with these 2 prs, W cls thro 2 prs, tw W twice, edge st and pin. (W is now on opposite side of work.)

Rep from * to * once.#

Rep from # to # for desired length, ending with half a repeat.

Care must be taken not to let this braid buckle or rise on the curves. If necessary, adjust the pinholes.

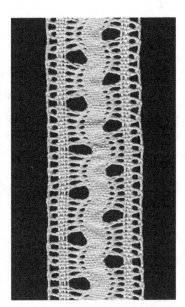

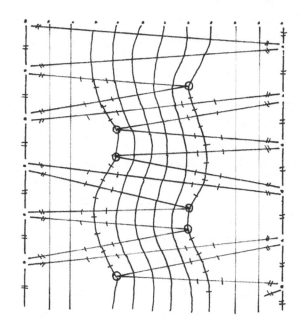

MEANDER WITH GROUND
14 prs

Work W from lt thro 2 prs in cls and tw, then 4 prs in cls. Work ts with W and next pr. Both these prs are now Ws and work out to each edge: the lt W thro 4 prs to lt, tw W once, cls and tw thro 2 prs, tw W once more, edge st and pin under 2 prs, and the rt W thro 2 prs to rt, tw W once, cls and tw thro 2 prs, tw W once more, edge st and pin. Leave.

Work 4th passive pr from lt thro 4 prs to rt in cls, tw once. Leave.

Work 3rd passive pr from lt thro same 4 prs to rt in cls, tw once. Leave.

Left side:
* Work W thro 2 prs in cls and tw, thro 3 prs in cls and ts with next pr.
Return with lt pr thro 3 prs in cls, tw W once, thro 2 prs in cls and tw, tw W once more, edge st and pin.*

Rep from * to * once more. Leave.

Right side:
Work W thro 4 prs in cls and tw, thro next 4 prs in cls, tw W once. Leave.
Take 4th pr from rt as new W and work to rt thro 2 prs in cls and tw, tw W once more, edge st and pin.
Return thro 3 prs in cls and tw, thro next 4 prs in cls, tw W once. Leave.
Take 4th pr from rt as new W and work to rt thro 2 prs in cls and tw, tw W once more, edge st and pin.

** W thro 2 prs to lt in cls and tw, thro 3 prs in cls, ts with next pr. Return with the rt of these 2 prs, cls thro 3 prs, tw W once, thro next 2 prs in cls and tw, tw W once more, edge st and pin.**

Rep from ** to ** once more.

Left side:
Work in similar manner to rt side.#

Rep from # to # for desired length.

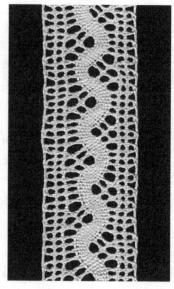

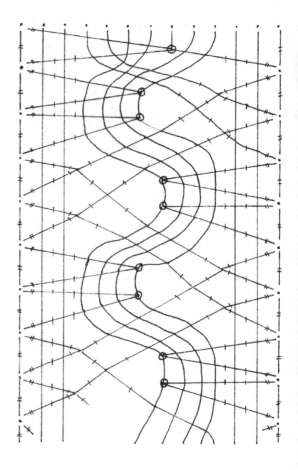

MEANDER WITH ROSE

17 prs

Work in cls throughout.

Work ts with W and 7th pr. Both these prs are now Ws. Work the lt W to the lt thro 6 prs, tw W twice, edge st and pin. Work rt W to rt thro 7 prs to rt, tw W twice, edge st and pin.

Work 5th passive pr from rt thro 5 prs to lt. Leave.

Work 4th passive pr from rt thro 5 prs to lt. Leave.

Rt W thro 3 prs to lt, return to rt with last pr passed thro, tw W twice, edge st and pin.

(Rt W thro 3 prs to lt, tw W once, thro 4 more prs, ts with next pr, return thro 4 prs, tw W once, thro 3 more prs, tw W twice, edge st and pin.) Rep once more. Leave.

* Left side:
W thro 3 prs, return to lt with last pr passed thro, tw W twice, edge st and pin.

Rose crossing with the 3rd, 4th, 5th and 6th passive prs from lt:
Tw each pr once.
2 lt prs cls and tw.
2 rt prs cls and tw.
2 centre prs cls and tw.
2 lt prs cls and tw.
2 rt prs cls and tw.
2 centre prs cls and tw.
2 lt prs cls and tw.
2 rt prs cls and tw.
Work the 2 rt prs thro 6 prs to the rt. Leave.

Lt W thro 3 prs, return with last pr passed thro, tw W twice, edge st and pin.

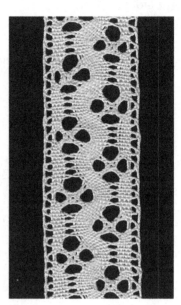

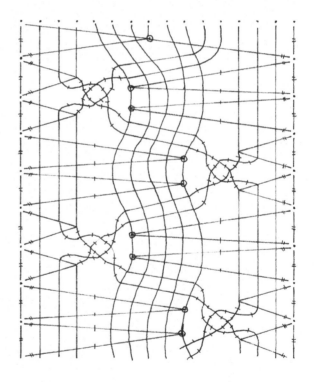

(W thro 3 prs, tw W once, thro 4 more prs, ts with next pr, return thro 4 prs, tw W once, thro 3 more prs, tw W twice, edge st and pin.) Rep once more.

Right side:
Work in similar manner to lt side.*

Rep from * to * for desired length.

MEANDER WITH SPIDER
16 prs

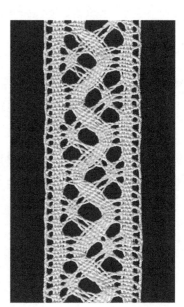

Work in cls throughout.

Work ts with W and 8th passive pr from lt. Both these prs are now Ws and work out to each edge: the lt W thro 7 prs to lt, tw twice, edge st and pin; and the rt W thro 5 prs to rt, tw twice, edge st and pin. Leave.

Work 5th passive pr from lt thro 4 prs to rt, tw once. Leave.
Work 4th passive pr from lt thro same 4 prs to rt, tw once. Leave.

Left side:
* Work W thro 3 prs, tw W once, thro 3 more prs, ts with next pr, return to lt with lt pr thro 3 prs, tw W once, thro 3 more prs, tw W twice, edge st and pin.*

Rep from * to * once more.

Work W thro 2 prs, ts with next pr, tw rt pr once, and return to lt with lt pr thro 2 prs, tw W twice, edge st and pin.
Work W thro 2 prs, tw once. Leave.

Right side:
Work W thro 2 prs to lt, ts with next pr, tw lt pr once and return with rt pr thro 2 prs, tw W twice, edge st and pin. W thro 2 prs tw once.

The spider is made with these 2 prs, which are twisted once, and the next 2 prs to the lt, which are also twisted once.

To work spider:
Lt 2 prs thro rt 2 prs, then outside lt pr thro next pr to rt, outside rt pr thro next pr to lt, cls with 2 centre prs, tw all 4 prs once. No pin is used. Pull up carefully, 2 lt prs are worked thro 4 prs to lt, tw both prs once. Leave.
Of the remaining spider legs, work the rt one thro 2 prs to rt, tw twice, edge st and pin. Return thro 2 prs.

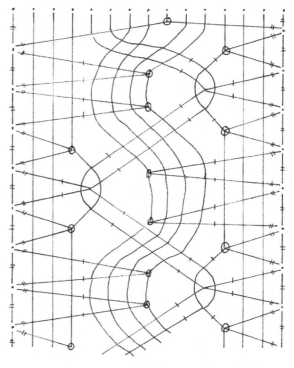

Take the remaining spider leg and work ts with next pr to the rt, thro 2 more prs, tw twice, edge st and pin.

** Return thro 3 prs, tw once, thro 3 more prs, ts with next pr. Return with rt pr thro 3 prs, tw once, thro 3 more prs, tw twice, edge st and pin.**

Rep from ** to ** once more.

Work W thro 2 prs, ts with next pr, tw lt pr once and return to rt with rt pr thro 2 prs, tw W twice, edge st and pin. Work W thro 2 prs, tw once. Leave.

Left side:
Work in similar manner to right side, beginning with a spider. #
Rep from # to # for desired length.

MESH - 1
16 prs

W should be on the rt of braid.

* W thro 2 prs in cls, tw W once, W thro next pr in cls and tw. (W thro next 2 prs in cls, tw all 3 prs once) Rep 3 more times. W thro next 2 prs in cls, tw W twice, edge st and pin.
Return thro 2 prs in cls, tw W once. Leave.
(Work cls with the next 2 prs to the rt) Rep 3 more times.
Work next pr in cls thro 2 prs to the rt, tw W twice, edge st and pin.*

Rep from * to * for desired length.

To finish: work the W from lt to rt in cls.

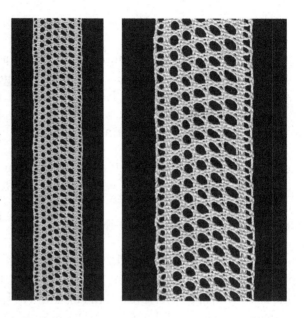

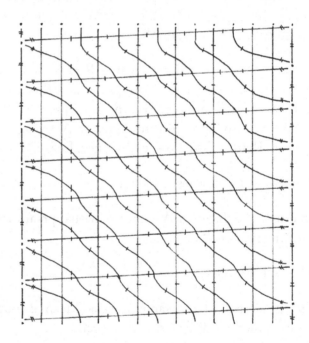

MESH - 2
16 prs

Work ts with W and centre pr. Both these prs are now Ws. Work lt W thro 6 prs to lt in cls, tw W twice, edge st and pin. Return thro 2 prs, tw W once. Leave.

Work rt W to rt in similar manner.

Counting from the lt: work 7th pr to the lt cls and tw thro 3 prs, cls thro 2 prs, tw W twice, edge st and pin. Return thro 2 prs, tw W once. Leave.
(Next 2 prs: cls and tw. Leave) Rep twice.

Counting from the lt: work 11th pr to the lt cls and tw thro 7 prs, cls thro 2 prs, tw W twice, edge st and pin. Return thro 2 prs, tw W once. Leave. (Next 2 prs cls and tw. Leave) Rep 3 more times. Next pr (4th pr from rt) works to the lt cls and tw thro 9 prs, cls thro 2 prs, tw W twice, edge st and pin. Return thro 2 prs, tw W once. Leave.

* (Next 2 prs cls and tw. Leave) Rep 3 more times. Counting from the rt: work 4th pr to the rt thro 2 prs, tw W twice, edge st and pin. Return thro 2 prs, tw W once, cls and tw thro 9 prs, cls thro 2 prs, tw W twice, edge st and pin. Return thro 2 prs, tw W once. Leave.*

Rep from * to * for desired length.

To finish: the diagonal Ws leave 2 twisted prs unworked until the braid is level.

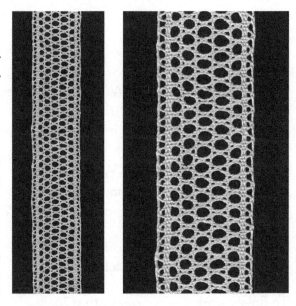

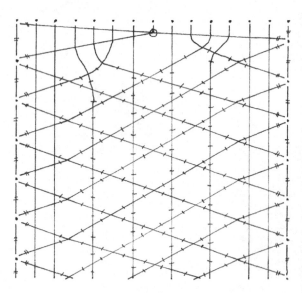

VARIATION 3:

This is started in the same way as Mesh 2, but the working method differs in two respects:
The passive prs are crossed in cls only (no tw).
The W is worked thro both prs in cls, then tw all 3 prs once.

VARIATION 4:

This is started in the same way as Mesh 2, but the working method differs in two respects:
The passive prs are crossed in cls only (no tw). The W works thro both prs in cls, tw W once, then cls and tw with the 2 prs passed thro.

MITTENS IN HALF STITCH
14 prs

Work ts with W and centre pr. Both these prs are now Ws.

Work lt W thro 5 prs to the lt in cls. Tw W twice, edge st and pin.
Work the same on other side with rt W.

* Work lt W thro 3 prs to rt in cls, tw W once, work W thro next 2 prs in hs, tw W once. Leave.
Work the same on the other side with rt W.

Two Ws in the centre: cls and tw twice.
Ws have now changed sides.

Work lt W to the lt thro 2 prs in hs and thro 3 prs in cls, tw W twice, edge st and pin. Leave.
Work the same on the other side with rt W.*

Rep from * to * for desired length.

To discard one W when returning to ordinary braid: make ts in the centre with the two Ws. The W will be the pr on the side of the next pinhole to be worked. The remaining pr becomes a passive.

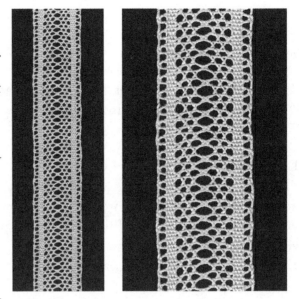

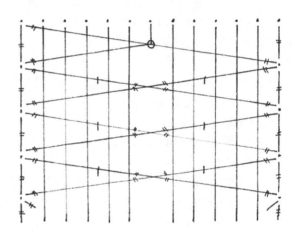

MOVEMENT

14 prs

Work in cls throughout.

Work ts with W and centre pr. Both these prs are now Ws. Work lt W to lt thro 5 prs, tw twice, edge st and pin. Work rt W to rt in similar manner.

* Lt W thro 2 prs, tw W once. Leave.
Rt W thro 8 prs, tw W once.
Cross the Ws with cls and tw, work the lt W thro 2 prs to lt, tw twice, edge st and pin, and the rt W thro 8 prs to rt, tw twice, edge st and pin.
Lt W thro 4 prs, tw W once. Leave.
Rt W thro 6 prs, tw W once.
Cross the Ws with cls and tw, and work lt W thro 4 prs to lt, tw twice, edge st and pin, and the rt W thro 6 prs to rt, tw twice, edge st and pin.
Lt W thro 6 prs, tw W once. Leave.
Rt W thro 4 prs, tw W once.
Cross the Ws with cls and tw, and work lt W thro 6 prs to lt, tw twice, edge st and pin, and rt W thro 4 prs to rt, tw twice, edge st and pin.
Lt W thro 8 prs, tw once. Leave.
Rt W thro 2 prs, tw once.
Cross the Ws with cls and tw, and work lt W thro 8 prs to lt, tw twice, edge st and pin, and rt W thro 2 prs to rt, tw twice, edge st and pin.
Lt W thro 6 prs, tw once. Leave.
Rt W thro 4 prs, tw once.
Cross the Ws with cls and tw, and work lt pr thro 6 prs to lt, tw twice, edge st and pin, and rt W thro 4 prs to rt, tw twice, edge st and pin.
Lt W thro 4 prs, tw W once. Leave.
Rt W thro 6 prs, tw W once.
Cross the Ws with cls and tw, and work lt pr thro 4 prs to lt, tw twice, edge st and pin, and rt W thro 6 prs to rt, tw twice, edge st and pin.*

Rep from * to * for desired length.

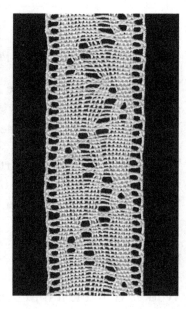

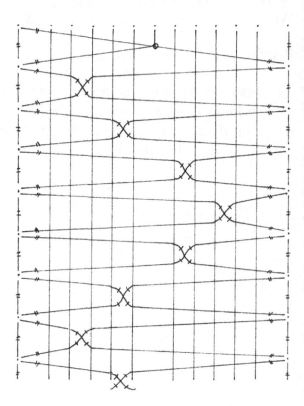

OPEN SPIDER

16 prs

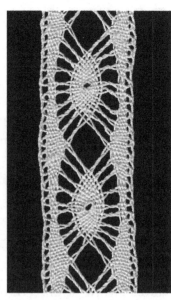

Work ts with W and centre pr. Both these prs are now Ws.
Work lt W to lt thro 6 prs, tw W twice, edge st and pin.
Leave.
Work rt W to rt in similar manner. Leave.

* Left side:
W thro 6 prs.
Tw W twice, leave, and return to lt with last pr passed
thro, tw W twice, edge st and pin. #
W thro 5 prs. Rep from # to #.
W thro 4 prs. Rep from # to #.
W thro 3 prs. Rep from # to #.
W thro 2 prs, tw W twice. Leave.

Right side:
Work in similar manner to lt side.

Centre 8 prs for open spider:
Work lt 4 prs thro rt 4 prs.
Work 4th pr from lt thro 3 prs, ts with next pr, return
to lt thro 3 prs, tw W twice, thro 2 more prs, tw W
twice, edge st and pin. Leave.
Work 4th pr from rt thro 3 prs, ts with next pr, return
to rt thro 3 prs, tw W, thro 2 more prs, tw W twice,
edge st and pin. Leave.
Work lt 4 prs thro rt 4 prs. Tw each pr twice. Leave.

Left side:
W thro 3 prs. Rep from # to #.
W thro 4 prs. Rep from # to #.
W thro 5 prs. Rep from # to #.

Right side:
Work in similar manner to lt side.*

Rep from * to * for desired length.

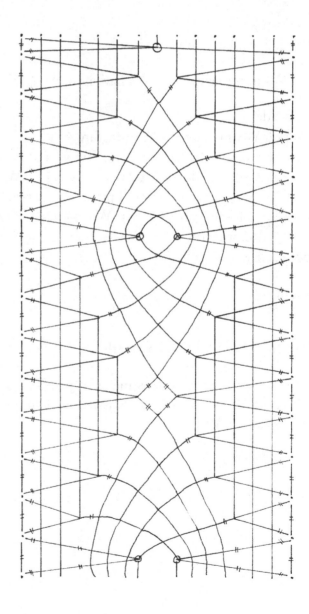

ORCHID - 1

16 prs

Work ts with W and centre pr. Both these prs are now Ws.
Work lt W to the lt thro 6 prs, tw W twice, edge st and pin.
Leave.
Work rt W to rt in similar manner.

* Centre 4 prs:
Work 2 lt prs thro 2 rt prs in cls.

Left side:
W thro 4 prs, tw W once, thro 2 more prs. Leave.

Right side:
Work in similar manner to lt side.

Cls Ws in the centre. The Ws have now changed sides.

Left side:
Work lt W thro 2 prs, tw W once, thro 4 prs, tw W twice,
edge st and pin. Return thro 4 prs. Tw W and next 2 prs
once and work W thro these 2 prs in cls and tw. Work the
lt of these 3 prs to the lt thro 4 prs in cls, tw twice, edge
st and pin. Return thro 4 prs, tw W once, cls and tw with
next pr. Return with the lt of these 2 prs thro 4 prs, tw W
twice, edge st and pin. Leave.

Right side:
Work in similar manner to lt side.*

Rep from * to * for desired length.

Finish with the centre crossing of 4 prs, then work ts
with both Ws. Leave 1 pr as a passive and continue with
the remaining W.

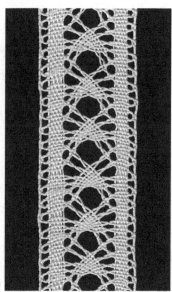

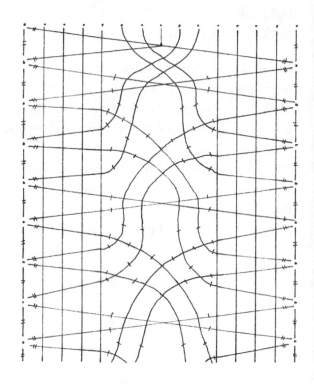

ORCHID - 2

16 prs

Work ts with W and centre pr. Both these prs are now Ws.
Lt W thro 6 prs to lt in cls, tw W twice, edge st and pin.
Work rt W to rt in similar manner.

* Centre 4 prs:
2 lt prs cls.
2 rt prs cls.
Work 2 lt prs thro 2 rt prs in cls.

Left side:
Work W thro 4 prs in cls, tw W once, thro 2 more prs.
Leave.

Right side:
Work in similar manner to lt side.

Cls W in the centre. The Ws have now changed sides.

Left side:
Lt W thro 2 prs to lt, tw W once, thro 4 more prs, tw
W twice, edge st and pin. Return thro 4 prs, tw W
and next 2 prs once, W thro next pr cls and tw. Return
with lt pr as new W, thro 4 prs, tw W twice, edge st
and pin. Leave.

Right side:
Work in similar manner to lt side.*

Rep from * to * for desired length.

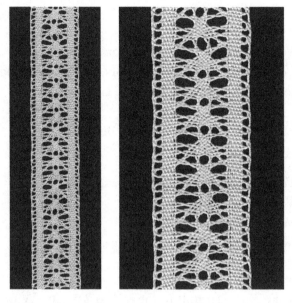

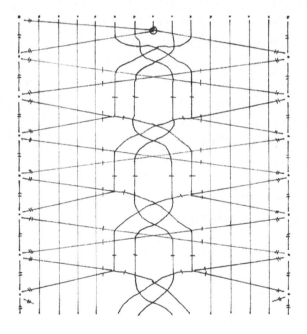

ORCHID - 3
16 prs

Work ts with W and centre pr. Both these prs are now Ws. Work lt W to lt in cls thro 6 prs, tw W twice, edge st and pin. Return thro 2 prs, tw W once. Leave.

Work rt W to rt in similar manner.

* Centre 4 prs:
Work 2 lt prs in cls thro 2 rt prs.
Work cls with 2 lt prs.
Work cls with 2 rt prs.
Tw all 4 prs once.

Left side:
Work 7th pr from lt to the lt thro 2 prs, tw W once, thro next pr in cls and tw, thro 2 more prs, tw W twice, edge st and pin. Return thro 2 prs, tw W once. Leave this pr and take next pr to rt (which has 1 tw) and work thro 2 prs to rt, tw W once, thro next pr in cls and tw. Return with lt of these 2 prs thro 2 prs, tw W once, thro next pr in cls and tw, thro 2 more prs, tw W twice, edge st and pin. Return thro 2 prs, tw W once. Leave this pr and take next pr to rt (which has 1 tw) and work thro 2 prs to rt, tw W once. Leave.

Right side:
Work in similar manner to lt side.*

Rep from * to * for desired length.

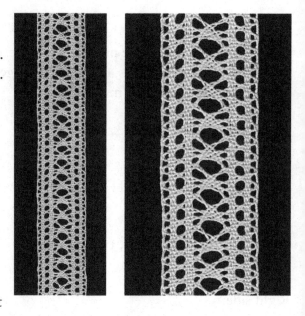

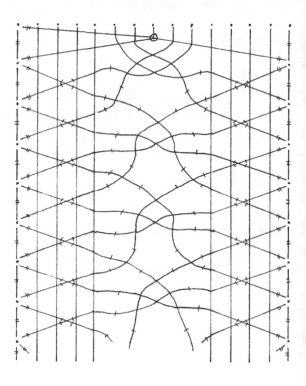

ORCHID - 4

16 prs

Work ts with W and centre pr. Both these prs are now Ws.
Work lt W to lt in cls thro 6 prs, tw W twice, edge st and
pin. Return thro 4 prs, tw W once. Leave.

Work rt W to rt in similar manner.

* Centre 2 prs:
Tw each pr twice and work 3 hs.

Centre 4 prs:
Tw the 2 outside prs once.
Work cls and tw with 2 lt prs.
Work cls and tw with 2 rt prs.
Work cls with 2 centre prs.

Left side:
Work W (6th pr from lt) to centre, cls and tw thro 1
pr and cls thro next pr.

Right side:
Work in similar manner to lt side.

Two Ws (centre prs) work cls. Both Ws have now
changed sides.

Left side:
Lt W to lt: cls thro 1 pr, tw W once, cls and tw thro
next pr, cls thro 4 prs, tw W twice, edge st and pin.
Return thro 4 prs, tw W once, cls thro next pr. Take
the lt of these 2 prs as new W, tw it once and work to
lt thro 4 prs, tw W twice, edge st and pin. Return thro
4 prs, tw W once. Leave.

Right side:
Work in similar manner to lt side.*

Rep from * to * for desired length.

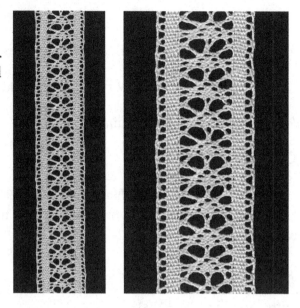

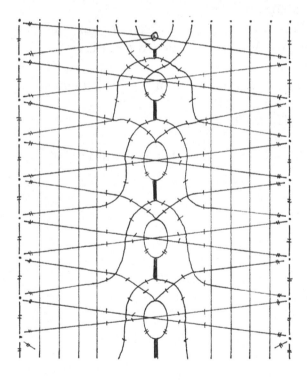

OVALS
14 prs

Work ts with W and centre pr. Both these prs are now Ws.

Lt W cls to lt thro 5 prs, tw W twice, edge st and pin. Leave.

Work rt W to rt in similar manner.

Centre 2 prs:
Cls and tw.

* Lt W cls thro 4 prs, tw W once, cls and tw thro next pr. Leave.

Work rt W in similar manner.

Centre 2 prs (i.e. the 2 Ws):
Cls and tw.
Work lt centre pr to lt, cls and tw thro one pr, cls thro 4 prs, tw W twice, edge st and pin. Leave.

Work rt centre pr to rt in similar manner.

Rep from * once more.

The whole pattern is then repeated from #.

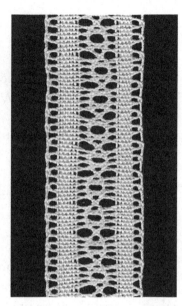

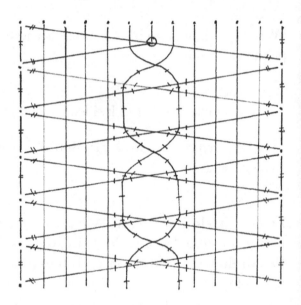

PEARL

14 prs

Work ts with W and centre pr. Both these prs are now Ws.
Work lt W to lt thro 5 prs, tw twice, edge st and pin.

Work rt W to rt in similar manner. Leave.

* Centre 2 prs:
Work cls st. Leave.
Work lt W thro 2 prs, tw W once, thro 3 prs.
Work rt W thro 2 prs, tw once, thro 3 prs.

Two Ws in the centre:
Cls and tw (Ws have changed sides).
Work lt W to lt thro 3 prs, tw W once, thro 2 prs, tw W
twice, edge st and pin. Leave.

Work rt W to rt in similar manner.*

Rep from * to *.

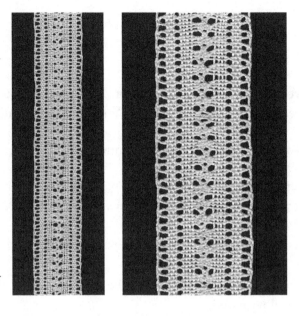

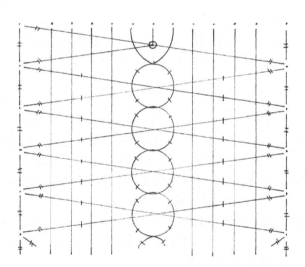

PERIWINKLE

16 prs

Work in cls throughout.

Work ts with W and centre pr. Both these prs are now Ws.
Work lt W thro 6 prs to lt, tw W twice, edge st and pin. Leave.

Work rt W to rt in similar manner.

Centre 6 prs:
Lt pr thro 1 pr to rt, ts with next pr, return with lt pr thro 1 pr. Leave.
Rt pr thro 1 pr to lt, ts with next pr, return with rt pr thro 1 pr. Leave.
Work the 2 centre lt prs thro the 2 centre rt prs.
Tw all 6 prs twice.

 Left side:
Counting from the lt, including edge pr, work 6th pr to lt thro 3 trail prs, tw W twice and work thro next pr. Leave.
Work 7th pr to lt thro 3 trail prs, tw W twice, work thro 2 more prs, tw W twice, edge st and pin. Leave.
Work 8th pr to lt thro 2 trail prs, ts with next pr, return with rt pr, thro 2 trail prs, tw W twice. Leave.
Work 2nd pr from lt thro 2 prs, tw W twice, thro 3 trail prs, tw W twice. Leave.
Work the 2nd and 3rd prs from lt in cls, and tw both prs twice. Work the rt of these 2 prs thro 3 trail prs to rt, tw W twice. Leave.
Work the 2nd pr from lt thro edge pr and pin.
Work the rt of these 2 prs thro 2 trail prs to rt, ts with next pr. Return with lt pr thro 2 trail prs, tw W twice, edge st and pin. Leave.

Right side:
Work in similar manner to lt side.

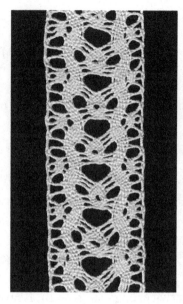

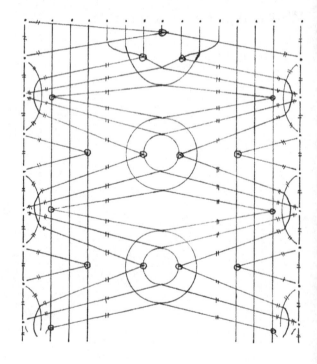

Open spider with centre 6 prs:
2 centre lt prs thro 2 centre rt prs.
Outside lt pr thro 1 pr to rt, ts with next pr, return with lt pr thro 1 pr.
Outside rt pr thro 1 pr to lt, ts with next pr, return with rt pr thro 1 pr.#
2 centre lt prs thro 2 centre rt prs.
Tw all 6 prs twice.*

Rep from * to * for desired length.

To finish, work the open spider from # to #.

Work Ws (second pr from lt and second pr from rt) to centre and make ts.
Turn diagram upside down for working method to finish.

PINWHEEL
14 prs

Work ts with W and centre pr: the lt pr cls thro 1 pr to lt and the rt pr cls thro 1 pr to rt.

Centre 2 prs:
Cls.

Tw 8 centre prs twice.

* Left side:
Take 6th pr from lt and work cls and 2 tw thro 2 prs to lt then cls thro 2 prs, tw W twice, edge st and pin. W cls thro 2 prs, tw W twice. Leave.

Take 7th pr from lt and work cls and 2 tw thro 3 prs to lt then cls thro 2 prs, tw W twice, edge st and pin. W cls thro 2 prs, tw W twice. Leave.

Right side:
Work in similar manner to lt side.

Centre 4 prs:
Lt 2 prs cross rt 2 prs in cls and 2 tw. Leave.

Centre of pinwheel is made as follows:

Left side:
Take 5th pr from lt and work cls and 2 tw thro 2 prs to rt. Leave.
Take 4th pr from lt and work cls and 2 tw thro 2 prs to rt. Leave.

Right side:
Work in similar manner to lt side.

Then 2 centre prs cls, the lt pr of these cls to lt thro 1 pr and the rt pr cls to rt thro 1 pr.

Two centre prs ts, the lt pr of these cls thro 1 pr to lt and the rt pr cls thro 1 pr to rt.

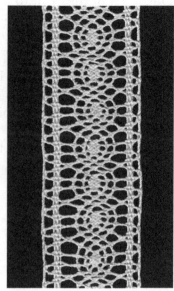

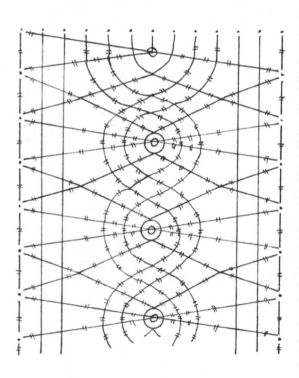

Centre 2 prs:
Cls.

Tw 4 centre prs twice.

Rep from * for desired length.

N.B. In the centre of the pinwheel cls may be worked instead of ts.

PLAID
15 prs

Work 3 rows of cls with edge st on each side.

* Leave W and edge prs.
Divide passives into 6 groups of 2 prs each and work 1 cls with each group.*

Work W thro 4 prs in cls, tw W twice, thro 4 prs in cls, tw W twice, thro 4 prs in cls, tw W twice, edge st and pin.
Rep last row going in opposite direction.

Rep from * to *.#

Work 3 rows of cls.

Rep from # to # for desired length.

VARIATION:

Vary the number of cls rows: see sample worked with 2 rows of cls.

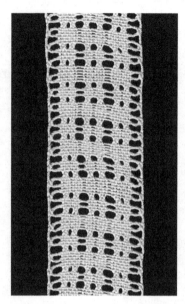

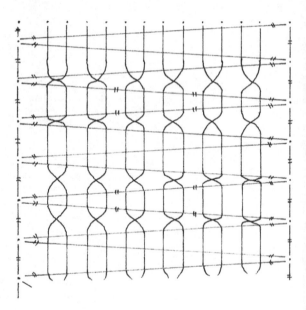

RIBBON

13 prs

Work 2 rows of cls.

Cross centre 8 passive prs in groups of 2 prs with cls.

* Work W thro 1 pr, tw W twice, W continues to work across in cls but tw W in the middle of each group of 2 prs and twice before the last passive, then tw W twice, edge st and pin.*

Centre 8 prs:
Tw once each.

Rep from * to *.

Leave W at edge.#

Rep whole pattern from # to # for desired length, finishing with the crossing of the 8 prs.

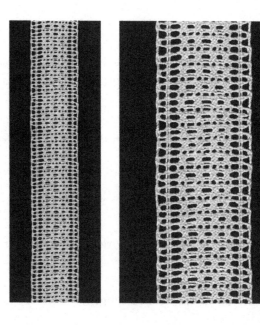

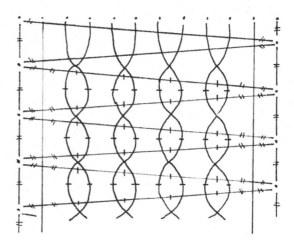

RICRAC

19 prs

* Work 4 rows of cls, finishing with W on lt. Leave edge pr and W on lt. Tw twice next 2 prs of passives. Leave.

Next 4 prs:
Pass lt 2 prs thro rt 2 prs in cls, tw each pr twice. Leave.#

Rep from # to # twice more, but no twists.

Tw last 2 passive prs twice.

Leaving the rt edge pr and working from the rt, rep from # to # 4 times.*

Rep from * and * for desired length.

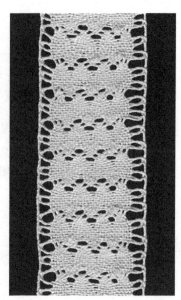

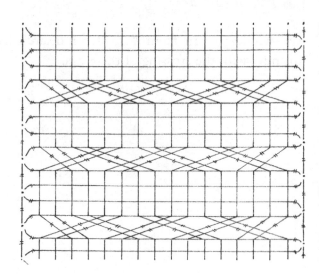

RINGLETS

14 prs

Work ts with W and centre pr. Both these prs are now Ws.

Left side:
Work the lt W to the lt thro 5 prs, tw twice, edge st and pin.
Work W thro 3 prs, tw W once. Leave. Take the last pr passed thro as new W and work it thro 2 prs to the lt, edge st and pin. Work back thro 2 prs, tw W once and work 2 hs with the next pr (small plait made).

Right side:
Work in similar manner to lt side.

* Centre 4 prs:
Cross the 2 lt prs thro the 2 rt prs in cls and tw.
2 lt prs work 2 hs.
2 rt prs work 2 hs.
(small plaits made)

Left side:
Work the 4th and 5th prs from the lt thro the 6th and 7th prs in cls. Tw each pr once and work 2 hs with each of the 4th and 5th prs and the 6th and 7th prs. Take the 4th pr from lt and work it to the lt, thro 2 prs, edge st and pin, and work back thro 2 prs. Leave. Take the 5th pr from lt and work it to the lt thro 3 prs, edge st and pin, and work back thro 2 prs, tw this pr and the next pr once and work 2 hs with them. Leave.

Right side:
Work in similar manner to left side.*

Rep from * to * for desired length.

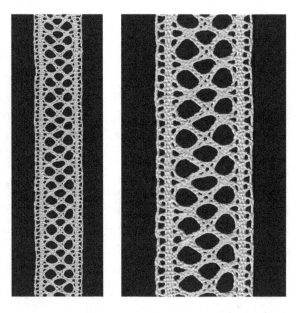

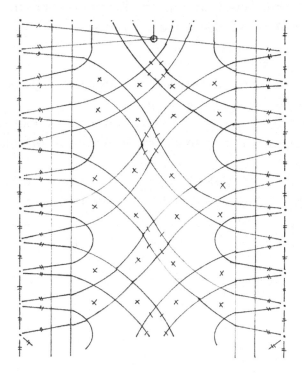

RIPPLES

16 prs

Work in cls throughout.

Work ts with W and centre pr. Both these prs are now Ws. Work lt W to the lt thro 6 prs, tw W twice, edge st and pin. Work rt W to the rt in a similar manner. Leave.

* Left side:
W thro 4 prs, tw W twice, thro 4 more prs, tw W twice, thro 3 more prs, ts with next pr. Return with lt pr thro 3 prs, tw W twice, thro 4 prs, tw W twice, thro 4 more prs, tw W twice, edge st and pin.
W thro 4 prs, tw W twice, thro 3 prs, ts with next pr. Return with lt pr, thro 3 prs, tw W twice, thro 4 more prs, tw W twice, edge st and pin.
W thro 3 prs, ts with next pr. Return with lt pr thro 3 prs, tw W twice, edge st and pin. Leave.

Right side:
W thro 3 prs, ts with next pr. Return with rt pr thro 3 prs, tw W twice, edge st and pin.
W thro 4 prs, tw W twice, thro 3 prs, ts with next pr. Return with rt pr thro 3 prs, tw W twice, thro 4 more prs, tw W twice, edge st and pin.
W thro 4 prs, tw W twice, thro 4 more prs, tw W twice, thro 3 more prs, ts with next pr. Return with rt pr thro 3 prs, tw W twice, thro 4 more prs, tw W twice, thro 4 more prs, tw W twice, edge st and pin. Leave.*

Rep from * to * for desired length.

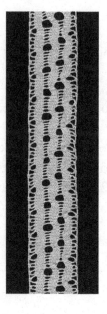
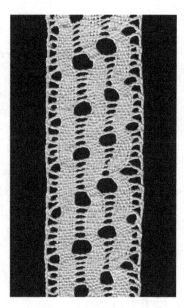

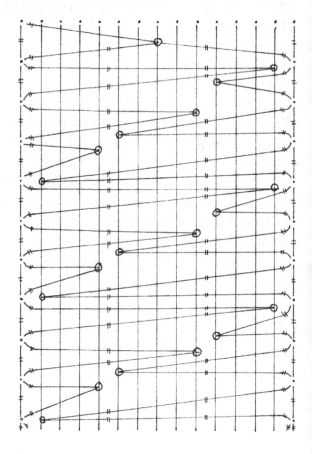

ROUNDABOUT - 1

14 prs

Work in cls throughout.

Work Ts with W and centre pr. Both these prs are now Ws. Work lt W to lt thro 5 prs, tw W twice, edge st and pin. Work rt W to rt in similar manner.

Centre 6 prs:
Work 3 lt prs thro 3 rt prs in cls. Leave.

Left side:
* W thro 2 prs, tw W once, thro 2 prs, ts with next pr. Take lt pr and work it to lt thro 2 prs, tw W once, thro 2 prs, edge st and pin.*
Rep from * to * once more.

Right side:
Work in similar manner to lt side.

Centre 6 prs:
Work 2 centre lt prs thro 2 centre rt prs.
Work outer lt pr thro 2 prs to rt, tw twice.
Work outer rt pr thro 2 prs to lt, tw twice.

Centre 2 prs:
Cls and tw twice.
Leave.

Left side:
Work W thro 2 prs, tw W once, thro 1 pr, ts with next pr. Return to lt with lt pr, thro 1 pr, tw W once, thro 2 prs, edge st and pin.

Right side:
Work in similar manner to lt side.

Centre 6 prs:
Lt centre pr thro 2 prs to lt.
Rt centre pr thro 2 prs to rt.

Centre 4 prs:
Cross lt 2 prs thro rt 2 prs.#

Rep from # to # for desired length.

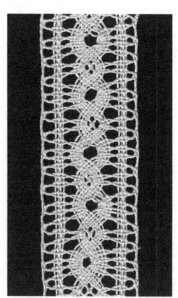

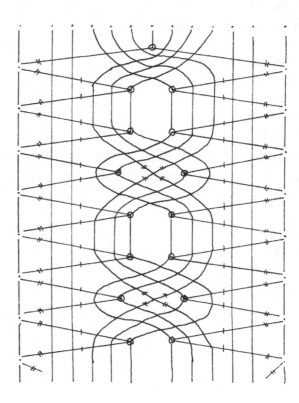

ROUNDABOUT - 2

14 prs

Work ts with W and centre pr. Both these prs are W. Work lt W to lt in cls thro 5 prs, tw W twice, edge st and pin. Work rt W to rt in similar manner.

* Centre 4 prs:
Tw each pr twice and work 2 lt prs thro 2 rt prs in cls, tw each pr twice. Leave.

Left side:
Work W thro 3 prs in cls, tw W once, cls and tw thro next pr, work ts with next pr. Take lt pr as W, tw it once, return to lt, cls and tw thro next pr, cls thro 3 prs, tw W twice, edge st and pin.

Right side:
Work in similar manner to lt side.

Centre 2 prs:
Tw each pr twice and work together in cls and tw twice.

Left side:
Work W thro 3 prs in cls, tw W once, cls and tw thro next pr, work ts with next pr. Take lt pr as W, tw it once and return to lt, cls and tw thro next pr, cls thro 3 prs, tw W twice, edge st and pin.

Right side:
Work in similar manner to lt side.*

Rep from * to * for desired length.

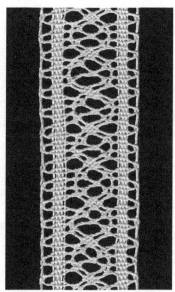

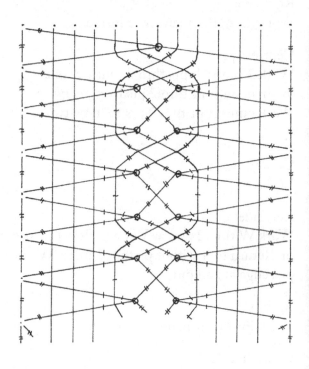

ROUNDABOUT - 3

14 prs

Work ts with W and centre pr. Both these prs are now Ws.
Work lt W to lt thro 5 prs, tw twice, edge st and pin.

Work rt W to rt in similar manner.

Centre 4 prs:
Work 2 lt prs thro 2 rt prs in cls. Tw each pr once.

* Left side:
Work lt W to the rt thro 5 prs in cls.

Right side:
Work rt W to lt thro 6 prs in cls. Ws have now changed sides.
Work new lt W to lt thro 5 prs, tw twice, edge st and pin.

Work new rt W to rt in similar manner.

Centre 4 prs:
Tw each pr once.*

Rep from * to * once more.#

Rep from # to # for desired length.

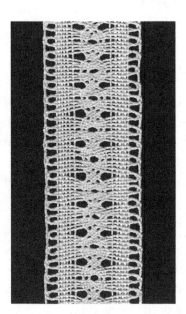

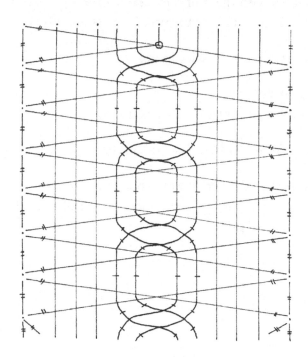

ROUNDEL - 1
16 prs

Work in cls throughout.

Work ts with W and centre pr. Both these prs are now Ws. Work the lt W to the lt thro 4 prs, tw twice, thro 2 more prs, tw twice, edge st and pin. Leave.

Work the rt W to the rt in a similar manner. Leave.

* Centre 4 prs:
Work the lt 2 prs thro the rt 2 prs in cls. Leave.

Left side:
Work W thro 2 prs, tw W twice, W thro 3 more prs, work a ts with the next pr.
Return with the lt of these 2 prs, thro 3 prs, tw W twice, thro 2 more prs, tw W twice, edge st and pin.#

Rep from # to # twice more.

Right side:
Work in a similar manner as lt side.*

Rep from * to * for desired length.

Note: If a thicker thread is being used on a wider braid, it may be better to twist once instead of twice between the passive prs.

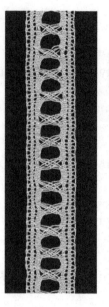
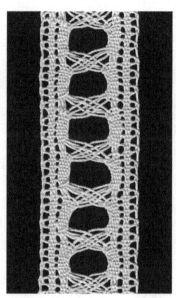

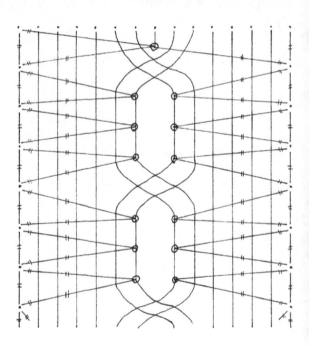

ROUNDEL - 2
16 prs

Work ts with W and centre pr. Both these prs are now Ws.
Work lt W thro 4 prs to lt, tw W twice, thro 2 more prs, tw
W twice, edge st and pin. Leave.

Work rt W to rt in a similar manner.

* Centre 4 prs:
2 lt prs cls. 2 rt prs cls.
Work 2 lt prs thro 2 rt prs in cls.
2 lt prs cls. 2 rt prs cls.

Left side:
(Work W thro 2 prs, tw W twice, thro 3 prs, ts with next
pr, return with lt pr thro 3 prs, tw W twice, thro 2 prs, tw
W twice, edge st and pin) Rep once more. Leave.

Right side:
Work in similar manner to lt side.*

Rep from * to * for desired length.

VARIATION:

The centre 4 prs may be twisted and worked with a
cls and tw, and the crossing made like a windmill,
i.e. using 2 bobbins together as 1 thread. This gives a
tighter appearance.

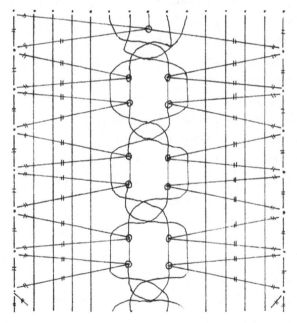

RUNNING RIVER

17 prs

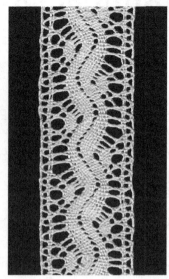

Work ts with W and 7th passive pr from lt. Both these prs are now Ws. Work lt W to the lt thro 6 prs, tw W twice, edge st and pin, and close pin with inside pr cls and tw twice. Leave. Work rt W to rt thro 7 prs, tw W twice, edge st and pin, and close pin with inside pr cls and tw twice.

W cls thro 3 prs to lt, tw W twice, thro 2 more prs, ts with next pr, return with rt pr thro 2 prs, tw W twice, thro 3 more prs, tw W twice, cls and tw twice, edge st and pin.

Close pin with cls and tw twice. Leave.

* Left side:

Work a 5 pr spider with prs 4, 5, 6, 7 and 8 from lt, in cls, following the diagram, making a ts with the prs that are ringed. On completion, pull up carefully; no pin is required. The 5 prs are then twisted twice.

Work the 4th pr from lt thro 3 prs to the lt in cls and tw twice, pin, and close pin.

Work the 5th pr from lt thro 4 prs to the lt in cls and tw twice, pin and close pin.

Work the 8th pr from lt thro (3 prs to rt in cls, tw W twice) Rep once more, thro the next 3 prs in cls and tw twice, pin, and close pin. Leave.

Work 7th pr from lt thro (3 prs to rt in cls, tw W twice) rep once more, thro the next 4 prs in cls and tw twice, pin, and close pin. Leave.

Work 6th pr from lt thro (3 prs to rt in cls, tw W twice) Rep once more. Leave.

Then work the 5th and 4th prs thro in the same way.

Work the 3rd pr from lt thro 3 prs to rt in cls, tw W twice, thro 2 more prs, ts with next pr. Return with lt pr thro 2 prs, tw W twice, thro 3 prs, tw twice, thro next 2 prs in cls and tw twice, pin and close pin. Leave.

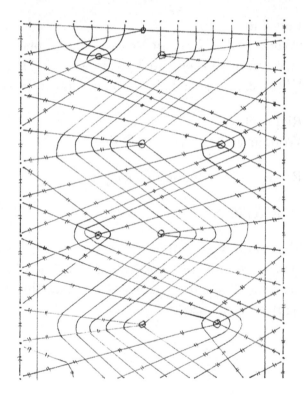

Lt spider

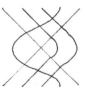

Rt spider

Right side:
Beginning with rt spider (see diagram) work in similar manner to lt side.*

Rep from * to * for desired length.

Finish with a spider on rt or lt and ts on the other side. Work Ws to centre and make ts, 1 pr continuing as W. If too tight, the inner footside pr may have one twist, or none as in the diagram.

Lt and rt spiders: these may be worked with cls in the centre instead of ts.

SIDESTEPS - 1
16 prs

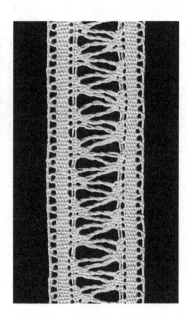

Work ts with W and 8th passive pr from lt. Both these prs are now Ws. Work lt W to lt thro 3 prs, tw W once, thro 4 prs, tw W twice, edge st and pin. Work rt W thro 5 prs to rt, tw W twice, edge st and pin.

Left side:
Work W in cls thro 4 passive prs, tw W once, cls thro next 2 prs and ts with next pr. Tw rt of these 2 prs twice, and the lt pr works another ts with the next pr to lt. Tw rt of these 2 prs twice, tw lt pr once and work it in cls thro next pr, tw it once again, work it thro remaining 4 passive prs, tw twice, edge st and pin. Leave.

* Right side:
All passive prs worked in cls.
Work W thro 4 passive prs, tw W once, thro next pr and ts with next pr (which has 2 twists).
Return with rt pr as W and work it thro next pr, tw W once, thro 4 prs, tw W twice, edge st and pin.
Return thro 4 prs, tw W once, thro 2 more prs and ts with next pr (the 2nd pr which has 2 twists). Tw lt pr twice. With the rt pr work another ts with next pr to rt, tw lt of these 2 prs twice, and tw rt pr once, work it thro 1 pr, tw it once again, thro 4 prs, tw twice, edge st and pin. Leave.

Left side:
Work in similar manner to rt side.*

Rep from * to * for desired length.

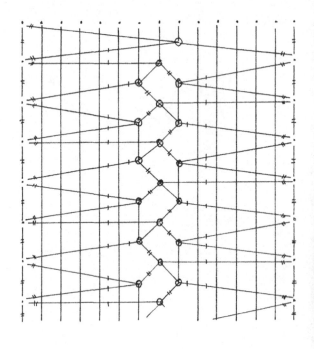

SIDESTEPS - 2
15 prs

Work ts with W and centre pr. Both these prs are now Ws. Work lt W to lt thro 5 prs, tw twice, edge st and pin. Work rt W to rt in similar manner.

Start from side of highest pinhole.

* Work W thro 5 prs, tw once, work cls with 6th (centre) pr, tw W once and centre pr 3 times. Return to edge with W.

Work the opposite side in similar manner.*

Rep from * to * for desired length.

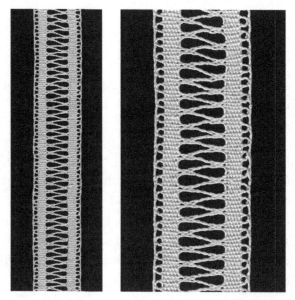

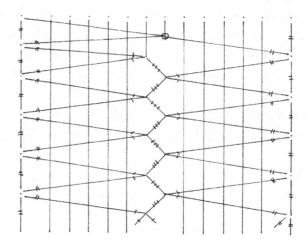

SIDESTEPS - 3
14 prs

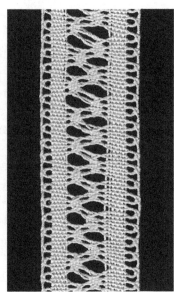

Work in cls throughout.

Work ts with W and 6th pr from rt and tw both prs once. Work the rt of these 2 prs thro 4 prs to rt, tw W twice, edge st and pin.

Work cls with the 6th and 7th prs from lt. Leave.
Work the lt pr from the ts to the lt thro 2 prs, tw W once, thro 4 prs, tw twice, edge st and pin. Work W thro 4 prs, tw W once, thro 2 prs, tw W once. Leave.
With 5th and 6th passive prs from lt work cls and tw once. Take the lt of these 2 prs and work it to the lt thro 4 prs, tw twice, edge st and pin.

* Right side of braid:
Work W (which is with the edge pr) thro 4 prs, tw W once, work cls and tw with next pr. Leave. Take the next pr on the lt and work it thro 2 prs to rt, tw it once, thro 4 prs and work edge st. Return thro 4 prs, tw W once, thro the next 2 prs, tw once and leave. With the last 2 prs passed thro (2 prs on the rt), work cls and tw. Take the rt of these 2 prs thro 4 prs, tw twice, edge st and pin. Leave.

Left side:
Work in similar manner to right side.*

Rep from * to * for desired length.

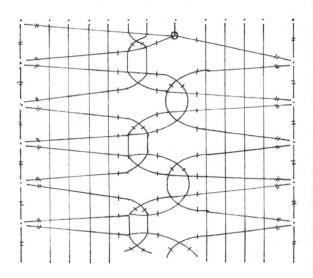

SIDESTEPS - 4
14 prs

Work in cls throughout.

Work ts with W and centre pr. Take the rt pr and work it to the rt thro 5 prs, tw twice, edge st and pin. Work back thro 2 prs. Leave. Take 6th pr from rt and work it to the rt thro 4 prs, tw twice, edge st and pin. Work back thro 2 prs. Leave.

Left side:
Take 7th pr from lt (the ts pr) and work it to the lt thro 5 prs, tw twice, edge st and pin. Work back thro 2 prs. Leave. Take 8th pr from lt and work it to the lt thro 6 prs, tw twice, edge st and pin. Work back thro 2 prs. Leave.

* Take prs 7 and 8 from lt, tw both of them once and work cls and tw. Work each of these 2 prs to the rt, edge st and pin, and back thro 2 prs. Leave.
Take prs 7 and 8 from lt, tw both of them once and work cls and tw. Work each of these 2 prs to the lt, edge st and pin and back thro 2 prs. Leave.*

Rep from * to * for desired length.

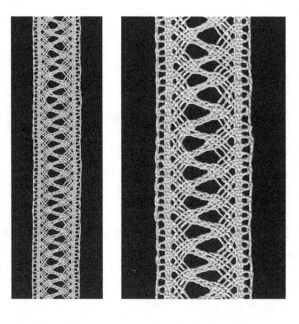

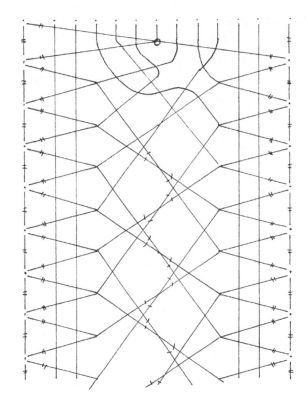

SNAKE
14 prs

Work ts with W and centre pr. Both these prs are now Ws.
Work lt W to lt thro 5 prs, tw W twice, edge st and pin.

Work rt W to rt in similar manner.

* Tw centre 6 prs once each. Divide them into 3 sets of 2 prs
and work each set with cls and tw once.
Work lt W to centre in cls.
Work rt W to centre in cls.
Cls both Ws in centre, then work them to the opposite edge
in cls and pin.

Centre 6 prs:
Tw each pr once.

Centre 4 prs:
Cross two lt prs thro 2 rt prs in cls and tw once.
Work lt Ws and rt Ws to the centre in cls, cross the two
Ws in cls and work them to the opposite sides in cls, and
edge st and pin.*

Rep from * to *.

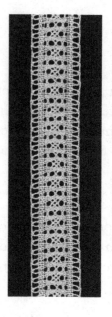
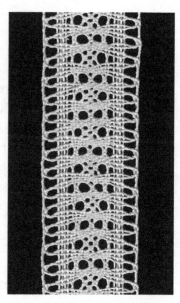

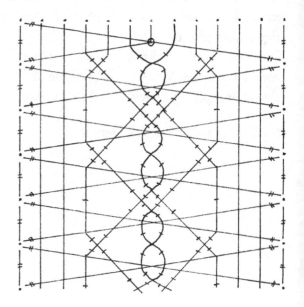

SPOT SPIDER

14 prs

Work in cls braid.

Leave W at rt side, count back and make hs with 6th and 7th passive prs. Work the lt of these 2 prs thro 4 prs to the lt, tw W twice, edge st and pin. Leave.
Cls two centre prs.

Left side:
Work W thro 4 prs to rt, tw last pr passed thro and work it back as new W thro 3 prs to lt, tw W twice, edge st and pin.
Work W thro 3 prs to rt. Leave.

Right side:
Work in similar manner to lt side.

Centre 6 prs:
Tw each pr twice.
Centre lt pr work thro 2 prs to lt in cls and tw.
Centre rt pr work thro 2 prs to rt in cls and tw.
Work spider with centre 4 prs. Tw each pr once.
Work 3rd pr from centre lt thro 2 prs to rt in cls and tw.
Work 3rd pr from centre rt thro 2 prs to lt in cls and tw.
Tw each 6 centre prs once more.

Note: a ts is made in the centre of the spider and no pin is used.

Centre 2 prs:
Cls. Leave.

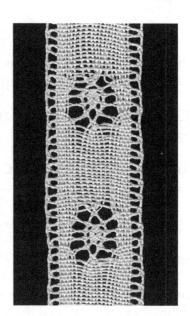

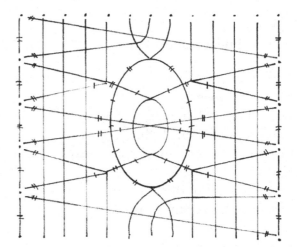

Right side:
Take 3rd pr from rt centre as W, work thro 3 prs to rt in cls, tw W twice, edge st and pin. Work W thro 4 prs to lt, tw last pr passed thro and work it back as new W thro 3 prs to rt, tw W twice, edge st and pin. Work W thro 4 prs to lt, tw W and next pr once and cross the 2 centre bobbins lt over rt (a reverse hs). Leave.

Left side:
Work in a similar manner to the rt side but omit reverse hs.

Work W thro all prs and continue braid for desired length.

STAR - 1
14 prs

Work ts with W and centre pr. Both these prs are now Ws and they work in cls throughout.

Work lt W to the lt thro 5 prs, tw W twice, edge st and pin. Leave.

Work rt W to the rt thro 5 prs, tw W twice, edge st and pin. Leave.

Tw 2 centre prs twice, cls. Leave.

* Left side:
W thro 4 prs. Leave W and return with last pr passed thro as new W, thro 3 prs, tw W twice, edge st and pin.
W thro 3 prs, leave W and return with last pr passed thro as new W, thro 3 prs, tw W twice, edge st and pin. Leave.

Right side:
Work in similar manner to lt side.

Centre 6 prs:
Tw each pr twice.
Centre lt pr work in cls thro 2 prs to lt.
Centre rt pr work in cls thro 2 prs to rt.
Work spider with centre 4 prs (ts may be used for centre 2 prs).
Work outside lt pr thro 2 prs to rt.
Work outside rt pr thro 2 prs to lt.
Tw 6 centre prs twice.
Cross 2 centre prs in cls.

Left side:
W thro 3 prs. Leave W and return with last pr passed thro as new W, thro 2 prs, tw W twice, edge st and pin. Leave.

Right side:
Work in similar manner to lt side.*

Rep from * to * for desired length.

STAR - 2
14 prs

Work in cls throughout.

Work ts with W and centre pr. Both these prs are now Ws.
Work lt W to lt thro 5 prs, tw W twice, edge st and pin.
Work back thro 2 prs (no tw). Leave.
Work rt W to rt in similar manner.

Centre 8 prs:
Work 4 lt prs thro 4 rt prs. Tw all 8 prs twice each.

Left side:
* Work 4th pr from lt thro 2 prs to lt, tw twice, edge st and pin, then back thro 2 prs. Leave (no twist).
Work 5th pr from lt thro 3 prs to lt, tw twice, edge st and pin, then back thro 2 prs only. Leave.
Work 6th pr from lt thro 4 prs to lt, tw twice, edge st and pin, then back thro 2 prs only. Leave.
Work 7th pr from lt thro 5 prs to lt, tw twice, edge st and pin, then back thro 2 prs only. Leave.*

Right side:
Rep from * to *, but count the prs from the rt.

The Spider:
Centre 8 prs:
Tw each pr twice. Work 4 lt prs thro 4 rt prs but make a ts with the centre prs, then cross the prs through one another again. Tw each pr twice.#

Rep from # to # for desired length.

To finish: work the first half of spider and make a ts with the 2 centre prs. Continue in cls with one of these prs as W.

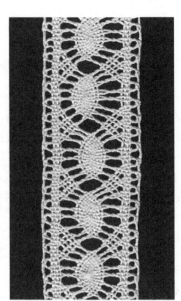

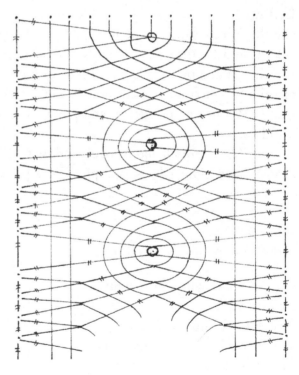

STAR - 3
14 prs

Work ts with W and centre pr.

Left side:
Work lt pr from the ts to lt thro 3 prs in cls, tw W once, cl and tw thro next 2 prs, tw W once more, edge st and pin. Work back thro 2 prs in cls and tw. Take the lt of these 2 prs to the lt and work cls and tw, tw W once more, edge st and pin, and work back thro 1 pr in cls and tw. Leave.

Right side:
Work in similar manner to lt side.

Centre 6 prs:
Work 3 lt prs thro 3 rt prs in cls. Tw each pr once.

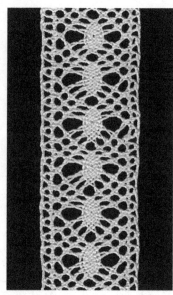

* Left side:
Take the 5th pr from lt (the lt of the centre 6 prs) and work cls and tw thro 3 prs to lt, tw W once more and work edge st and pin. Close pin with cls and tw.
Take the 6th pr from lt and work cls and tw thro 4 prs to lt, tw W once more, edge st and pin. Close pin with cls and tw.
Take the 7th pr from lt and work cls and tw thro 5 prs to lt, tw W once more, edge st and pin. Close pin with cls and tw. Leave.

Right side:
Work in similar manner to lt side.

Spider crossing with centre 6 prs:
Work in cls:
Work 3 lt prs thro 3 rt prs.
Work lt centre pr thro 2 prs to lt.
Work rt centre pr thro 2 prs to rt.
Centre 4 prs:
Work lt 2 prs thro 2 rt prs.
Tw each pr once*

Rep from * to * for desired length.

STRIPES
16 prs

* Work 2 rows of cls, leaving W and edge pr on lt.

From lt:
(Next 2 prs of passives cls and tw) Rep 5 more times. Tw last pr passives once.

From the rt:
Leave the rt edge pr. (Next 2 prs of passives work cls) Rep 5 more times.*

Rep from * to * for desired length.

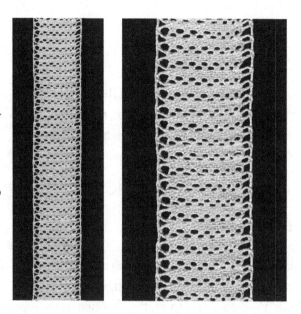

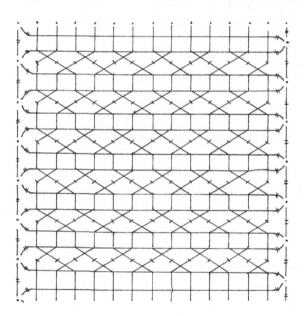

TIFFANY

14 prs

Work in cls throughout.

Work ts with W and centre pr. These 2 prs are now Ws. Work lt W to lt thro 3 prs, tw W once, thro 2 prs, tw W twice, edge st and pin. Work rt W to rt in similar manner.

* Centre 4 prs:
Work 2 lt prs thro 2 rt prs in cls.

Left side:
Work W thro 2 prs, tw W once, thro 2 prs, ts with next pr. Take the lt of these 2 prs and work to the lt thro 2 prs, tw W once, thro 2 prs, tw W twice, edge st and pin.
Work W thro 2 prs to rt, tw W once, thro 1 pr, ts with next pr. Take the lt of these 2 prs and work to lt thro 1 pr, tw W once, thro 2 prs, tw W twice, edge st and pin. Leave.

Right side:
Work in similar manner to lt side.

Centre 2 prs:
Tw each pr twice, work cls and 2 tw. Leave.

Left side:
Work W thro 2 prs, tw W once, thro 2 prs, ts with next pr. Take the lt of these 2 prs and work to the lt thro 2 prs, tw W once, thro 2 prs, tw W twice, edge st and pin.*

Rep from * to * for desired length.

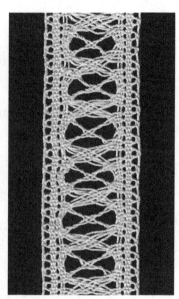

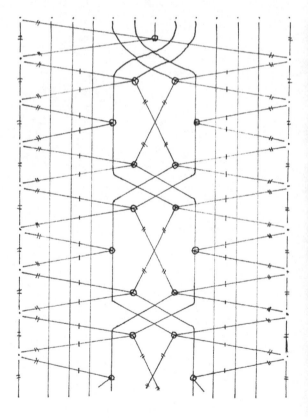

TORQUE - 1
14 prs

Work ts with W and centre pr and tw both prs once. Work the lt of these 2 prs in cls thro 5 prs to lt, tw W twice, edge st and pin, and return thro 2 prs. Leave.

Work the rt of the centre prs to the rt in similar manner.

Centre 2 prs:
Tw once and work cls and tw. Work the lt of these 2 prs to the lt thro 5 prs, tw W twice, edge st and pin, return thro 2 prs. Leave.

Work rt centre pr to the rt in similar manner.

Centre 4 prs:
Using each pr as one thread work 3 hs (small plait made).

Centre 2 prs:
Work together in cls and tw.

Left side:
* Work 6th pr from edge to the lt, work edge st and back thro 2 prs. Leave.
Work 7th pr from edge to the lt, work edge st and back thro 2 prs. Leave.*

Right side:
Work in similar manner to lt side from * to *.#

Rep from # to # for desired length.

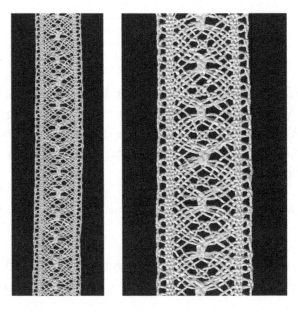

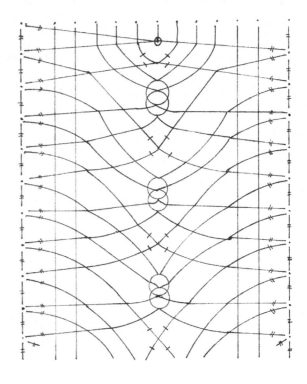

TORQUE - 2
14 prs

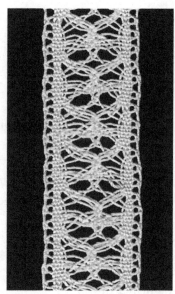

Work cls throughout.

Work ts with W and centre pr. Both these prs are now Ws.
* Work lt W to lt thro 5 prs, tw W twice, edge st and pin.
Work W thro 3 prs, ts with next pr, and work back with lt pr
thro 3 prs, tw W twice, edge st and pin, and work W back thro
2 prs. Leave (no tw).

Work rt W to rt in similar manner.

Centre 2 prs:
Tw each pr once and work together with cls and tw.
Work lt pr to lt thro 5 prs, tw W twice, edge st and pin. Leave.

Work rt pr of the 2 centre prs in similar manner. Leave.

Centre 4 prs:
Use each pr as one thread and work 2 hs. Take the 2 centre
prs and work cls and tw. Leave.
Work the rt and lt Ws to the centre and make a ts.*

Rep from * to * for desired length.

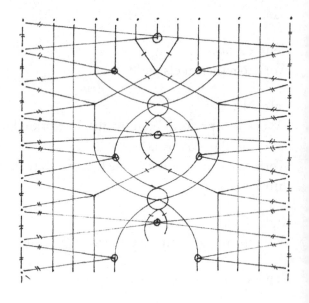

TRELLIS
14 prs

Work ts with W and centre pr. Both these prs are now Ws.
Work lt W to lt in cls thro 5 prs, tw W twice, edge st and
pin. W thro one pr in cls. Leave.
Work rt W to rt in similar manner.

* Divide centre 8 prs into two groups:

Lt group of 4 prs:
Cross lt 2 prs thro rt 2 prs in cls.
Tw all 4 prs twice.

Two lt prs both work out to lt edge, one at a time: the first
(i.e. the lt) pr thro 2 prs in cls, tw twice, edge st and pin,
return thro one pr. Leave. Then work the second pr thro 3
prs in cls, tw twice, edge st and pin. Return thro one pr.
Leave.

Rt group of 4 prs:
Work in similar manner to lt group.

Centre 4 prs:
Cross 2 lt prs thro 2 rt prs in cls.

Centre 8 prs:
Tw each pr twice. *

Rep from * to * for desired length.

One tw instead of two may be used between the
crossings for a less open effect.

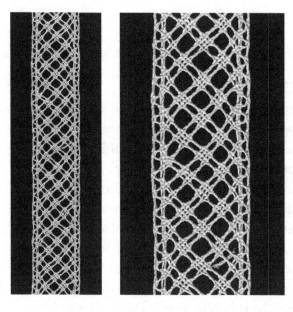

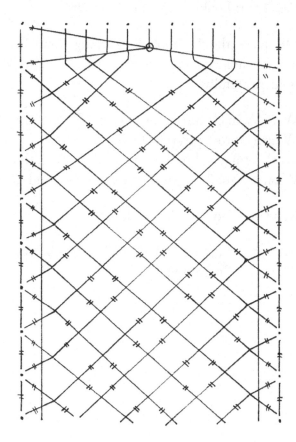

TWIST
15 prs

Work 1 or 2 rows of cls with edge st, leaving Ws on the lt.

* Centre 6 prs:
Using the bobbins singly, these are flipped thus:
Pass the rt bobbin over 11 bobbins to lt.
Pass the rt bobbin over 10 bobbins to lt.
Pass the rt bobbin over 9 bobbins to lt.
Pass the rt bobbin over 8 bobbins to lt.
Pass the rt bobbin over 7 bobbins to lt.
Pass the rt bobbin over 6 bobbins to lt.
Pass the rt bobbin over 5 bobbins to lt.
Pass the rt bobbin over 4 bobbins to lt.
Pass the rt bobbin over 3 bobbins to lt.
Pass the rt bobbin over 2 bobbins to lt.
Pass the rt bobbin over 1 bobbin to lt.

OR place the 12 bobbins, keeping them in order, on a stitch holder and turn them over. Remove the stitch holder carefully.

Work W in cls thro 3 prs to rt, tw W once, thro 6 prs, tw W once, thro 3 prs, tw W twice, edge st and pin.
Work W in cls thro 3 prs to lt, tw W once, thro 6 prs, tw W once, thro 3 prs, tw W twice, edge st and pin.*

Rep from * to * for desired length.

Note: More than two rows of cls can be worked between the twists if preferred.

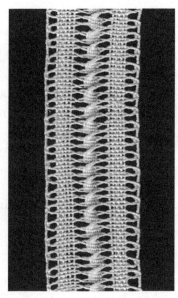

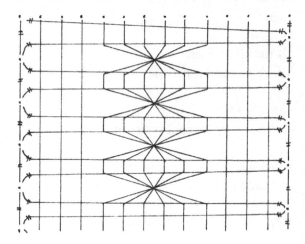

VIOLA

14 prs

Work in cls throughout.
Work ts with W and centre pr.
Work lt pr thro 1 pr to lt and work rt pr thro 1 pr to rt.
Work cls with the 2 centre prs and tw all 4 prs once. Leave.

Work cls and tw with 2 prs on the lt of the 4 centre prs.
Work cls and tw with 2 prs on the rt of the 4 centre prs.

* Left side:
Leave edge pr and 2 passive prs. Take the next 4 prs (which
have 1 tw) and work the lt 2 prs thro the rt 2 prs in cls. Tw
all 4 prs once. Take the lt of these 4 prs and work it to the
lt thro 2 prs, tw twice, edge st and pin. Return thro 2 prs,
tw W once and work thro next pr in cls and tw. Leave.

Right side:
Work in similar manner to lt side.

Centre 4 prs:
Work 2 lt prs thro 2 rt prs in cls. Tw all 4 prs once.

Rep from * for desired length.

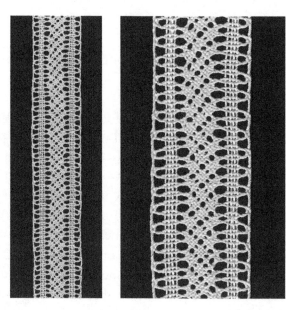

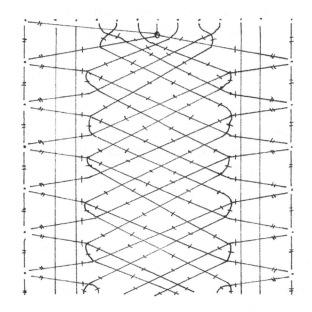

WAVES
16 prs

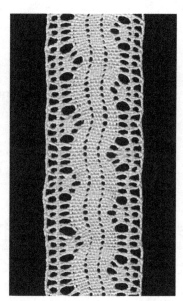

Work in cls throughout. W from lt thro 1 pr, cls and tw. Leave.

From right side:
3rd and 4th prs from rt, cls. Lt of these 2 prs (thro 3 prs to lt, tw W once) Rep twice more, thro 1 pr. (These 2 prs will form the body of the little spider). Leave.
* Tw once 3rd pr from rt and work it to the rt thro 1 pr in cls and tw, tw W once more, edge st and pin. Return thro inner edge pr in cls and tw, then (thro 3 prs to lt, tw W once) rep once more, thro 2 prs, ts with next pr.
With the lt of these 2 prs tw once, work thro 2 prs (for the little spider) tw W once, thro next pr, cls and tw, tw W once more, edge st and pin. Return thro inner edge pr cls and tw, thro 2 spider prs, tw W once. Leave.
Take the next pr (which was the rt pr from the ts) and work it to the rt thro 2 prs, tw W once (thro 3 prs, tw W once) rep once more, thro 1 pr in cls and tw, tw W once more, edge st and pin. Return thro inner edge pr in cls and tw, then (thro 3 prs to lt, tw W once) rep once more, thro 2 prs, ts with next pr.
Work the rt of these 2 prs thro 2 prs to rt, tw W once (thro 3 prs, tw W once) rep once more, thro 1 pr in cls and tw, tw W once more, edge st and pin. Return thro inner edge pr in cls and tw. Leave.

From left side:
Beginning with 3rd and 4th prs from lt, cls and tw.
Work rt of these 2 prs (thro 3 prs, tw W once) rep twice more. Work cls with next pr. Leave. (These 2 prs will form the body of the little spider.)

Now work in same way in reverse as rt side from.*

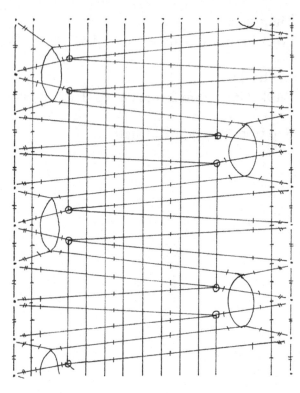

WHISKERS - 1
14 prs

Work ts with W and centre pr. Both these prs are now Ws. Work lt W to lt thro 3 prs, tw W once, thro 2 prs, tw W twice, edge st and pin. Leave.

Work rt W to rt in similar manner.

* Centre 2 prs:
Tw both prs once and work 3 hs (small plait made). Leave.

Left side:
Work W thro 2 prs, tw W once, thro 2 prs, leave the W and take the last pr passed thro as new W and work it to the lt thro 1 pr, tw W once, thro 2 prs, tw W twice, edge st and pin. Work W to rt thro 2 prs, tw W once, thro 2 prs. Leave.

Right side:
Work in similar manner to lt side.

Centre 4 prs:
Work cls with 2 lt prs.
Work cls with 2 rt prs.
Work cls with 2 centre prs.
Work cls with 2 lt prs.
Work cls with 2 rt prs.

Take the lt of the 4 centre prs as W and work it thro 2 prs to lt, tw once, thro 2 prs, tw twice, edge st and pin. Take the rt of the 4 centre prs as W and work in similar manner to rt.*

Rep from * to * for desired length.

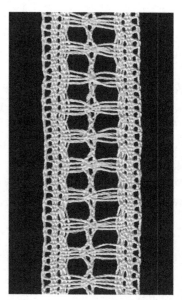

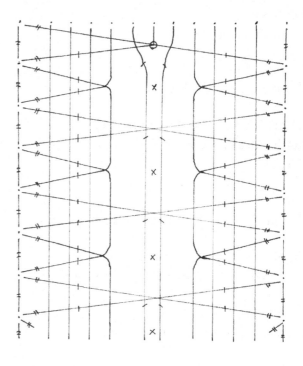

WHISKERS - 2
14 prs

Work in cls throughout.

Work ts with W and centre pr. Both these prs are now Ws. Work lt W to lt thro 5 prs, tw W twice, edge st and pin.

Work rt W to rt in similar manner.

Centre 2 prs:
Tw each pr twice. Leave.

Left side:
Work W thro 4 prs, tw W twice. Take the last pr passed thro as new W and work it to lt thro 3 prs, tw twice, edge st and pin. Leave.

Right side:
Work in similar manner to lt side.

* Centre 4 prs:
Work 2 lt prs thro 2 rt prs. Leave.

Left side: Work W thro 5 prs to rt.
Right side: Work W thro 6 prs to lt. (Ws have changed sides.)

Left side:
W thro 5 prs to lt, tw twice, edge st and pin.

Right side:
W thro 5 prs to rt, tw twice, edge st and pin.

Centre 4 prs:
Work 2 lt prs thro 2 rt prs. Tw each pr twice. Leave.

Left side:
Work W thro 4 prs to rt. Take last pr passed thro as new W and work it to the lt thro 3 prs, tw twice, edge st and pin. Work W thro 5 prs to rt. Leave.

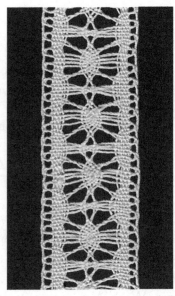

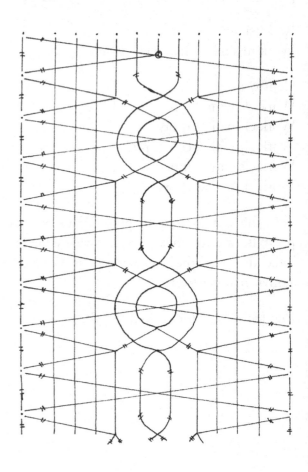

Right side:
Work W thro 4 prs to lt. Take last pr passed thro as new W and work it to the rt thro 3 prs, tw twice, edge st and pin. Work W thro 6 prs to lt.
Ws have now changed sides.

Left side:
Work lt W to lt thro 5 prs, tw twice, edge st and pin. Work W thro 4 prs to rt and tw it twice. Take the last pr passed thro as new W and work to lt thro 3 prs, tw twice, edge st and pin. Leave.

Right side:
Work in similar manner to lt side.*

Rep from * to * for desired length.

ZIGZAG HOLES

14 prs

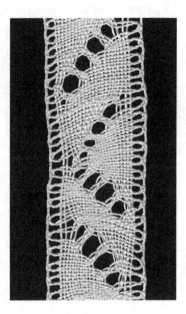

Left side:

* Work W thro 10 passive prs, leaving the last pr and edge pr. Work 1 cls with the last 2 prs passed thro, then work 1 cls with the rt pr and the W. Leave these 2 prs. Take the pr on the lt as the new W and work to the lt thro 8 prs, tw W twice, edge st and pin.

Rep from *, leaving out 2 more prs each time until 4 sets of 2 prs have been left out, leaving the W as the fourth pr from the lt.

Right side:

Take the 3rd pr from rt (i.e. the rt pr of the first set) as W and work to rt thro 1 pr, tw W twice, edge st and pin.

** Return thro 4 prs, take the last pr passed thro as new W and return thro 3 prs to rt, tw W twice, edge st and pin.

Rep from **, adding 2 prs each time until three more sets have been taken in.

Zigzag holes:

Work the new W thro to the rt edge before commencing the same pattern in reverse on the opposite side.

Holes sloping in the same direction:

Any number of cls rows may be worked before recommencing the pattern. In the sample shown the pattern is continuous.

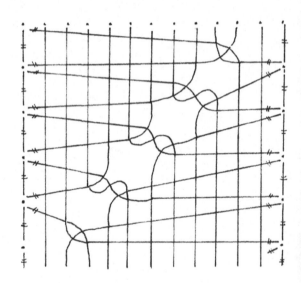

Index

Made in the USA
Las Vegas, NV
19 September 2023

77787682R00083